Target Heaven

What You Didn't Know About Father Benedict Groeschel

Good Counsel Homes

En Route Books and Media, LLC
St. Louis, MO

⊛ENROUTE
Make the time

En Route Books and Media, LLC
5705 Rhodes Avenue
St. Louis, MO 63109

Cover credit: Good Counsel Homes

ISBN-13: 979-8-88870-012-9
Library of Congress Control Number: 2022950816

Copyright © 2014, 2022 Good Counsel Homes
Originally published as *Father Benedict Groeschel: A Conversational Biography*

No part of this booklet may be reproduced, stored in a retrieval system, or transmitted in any form, or by any means, electronic, mechanical, photocopying, or otherwise, without the prior written permission of the author. All rights reserved.

Table of Contents

Introduction: Mother Agnes, Superior, Sisters of Life 1

Chapter 1: Interview with Marjule Drury—Father Benedict Groeschel's sister 9

Chapter 2: Interview with Christopher Bell 39

Chapter 3: Interview with Dr Ann Marie Wallace 57

Chapter 4: Interview with Father John Lynch 75

Chapter 5: Interview with Father Andrew Apostoli, CFR 123

Chapter 6: Interview with Father Benedict Groeschel, CFR 135

Epilogue: Father Fidelis Moscinski, CFR 161

Father Benedict Groeschel's Books 167

Introduction
Mother Agnes Mary Donovan, SV
Superior, Sisters of Life

Mother Agnes is one of eight original members who formed the Sisters of Life under the direction of John Cardinal O'Connor of New York in 1991. Mother Agnes is a former school psychologist and was a professor at Columbia

University prior to entering religious life. The following is excerpted from her speech at Father Benedict's 50th Anniversary celebration on Sunday, October 18, 2009.

Father Benedict, thank you for letting us celebrate. I suspect this is a little hard for you, but it is a blessing for us to be able to celebrate the priesthood and your fidelity during all of these 50 years. I have the joy of being able to say a few words about you, and what comes to mind are the words: priest, prophet, and king.

Father Benedict has certainly participated in the priesthood of Our Lord and Savior Jesus Christ as a priest, prophet, and king.

I think an apt patron for you, Father Benedict, might be St. John the Baptist whose job it was to **Prepare ye the way of the Lord**. Through the years, Father Benedict has counseled many, beginning at Children's Village in Dobbs Ferry, New York. He has served priests, seminarians, and countless others at Trinity Retreat House in Larchmont, New York. With his blessed intuition and the gift of his learning, he has led us to a better understanding of our humanity and then to our God, who shared that humanity.

On a personal note, during the summer the Sisters of Life were founded, Father Benedict invited the eight of us over to Trinity Retreat House. He said we would have a Mass and a barbeque. I had only read his books. I was not much of a television viewer, so I really didn't know what a personality he was.

So we went and had a beautiful Mass inside the chapel at Trinity. We ate a wonderful meal and then went on a lovely walk on the Long Island shore. At one point during our walk, he took me aside just for 30 seconds, looked at me, and said, "Sister, this will be a very difficult undertaking, and I want you to know I'll be there for you."

I thought to myself, "So what's so difficult?" But I'll tell you, it wasn't very long after that I began to understand what some of the difficulties would be, and Father Benedict was true to his word. Whether it was ten at night or four in the morning, Father Benedict would be there, and he would answer the phone and see someone in distress.

Thank you, Father Benedict. The Sisters of Life are here because, in no small part, you were there for us.

A prophet. Father Benedict has forcefully proclaimed the Word to the world through his books, his preaching, and through EWTN. He has proclaimed the Word in a thousand ways to all of us who needed hope. He has guarded the Church and the treasures of its grace. We really can't imagine the millions who have listened to him and who have been blessed.

We had one really striking experience at Sacred Heart, where we care for and have young pregnant women live with us. Julie was a young girl who grew up in Brooklyn in the midst of great poverty. But really, the greatest poverty was within her home, where there was tension, sorrow, and terrible fighting between her parents.

One night as the fighting escalated, she returned to her room and to the television just to block out the noise and fright of hearing her parents fight. She was surfing through the channels, and she happened to stumble upon Father Benedict, who at that moment said, "God loves you."

Who knows what the theme of his show was, but for Julie, it was a profound moment of grace, and she realized, even though her parents were incapable of properly showing it, God did love her. She hung on through a rough adolescence because of those words, and she would look for this bearded Friar on television even though she did not even know his name. In essence, Father Benedict became like a father to her.

And then one day, when Julie was living with us at Sacred Heart, Father Benedict walked into our convent for a meeting, and Julie saw him. She ran over to one of our sisters very excitingly asking, "Who is that? Who is that?"

And the sister responded, "That's Father Benedict."

Julie went through a whole series of questions and asked, "Is he on TV sometimes?" And she came to discover that this was the same Friar whom she had known as a little girl.

As the meeting concluded, our sisters brought Julie over to Father Benedict. He blessed her and her unborn baby. Several months later, Father Benedict came and Baptized Julie's little boy, whom she named Sebastian.

For many of us, Father Benedict, we have not surrendered to fear because of you. You have challenged us, and you have stood with us. You have led us forward to live our faith in joy and in courage. You have stirred our lagging hope and faith. By the witness of your life, you have challenged us to be who we are: the Church Militant, which means the people of God, called forth in grace to engage on the earth in the fight between good and evil.

For those of you familiar with J.R.R. Tolkien's *The Lord of the Rings*, I think of you, Father Benedict, when I hear the words of Aragorn, who summoned those of Rohan to engage the definitive battle for Middle Earth. He said:

> My brothers! I see in your eyes the same fear that would take the heart of me. A day may come when the courage of men fails, when we forsake our friends and break all bonds of fellowship, but it is not this day. An hour of woes and shattered shields, when the age of men comes crashing

down! But it is not this day! This day we fight! By all that you hold dear on this good Earth, I bid you stand, Men of the West!

Father Benedict, how many times have we said in the face of fear and difficulty, it is not this day because we are blessed to have you with us. Thank you!

Chapter 1
Marjule Drury

Marjule Drury, born Marjule Groeschel, is one of six children in Father Benedict's family. Marjule, a native of Caldwell, New Jersey, was kind enough to talk about her family life and her very famous brother on April 20, 2009.

Q: Marjule, you have a very interesting name. How did it come to be?

Marjule: It's Margaret and Julia. It's my mother's two Great Aunts' names. My grandmother put the names together for Marjule, which was also my mother's name.

Q: Do you know anyone else with the name?

Marjule: Well, I named my daughter Marjule and my niece has it as well. I didn't think the name existed anywhere else until after my brother Ned passed away. I heard from a woman whose husband worked with him. She saw the obituary and contacted me when she saw my name. She was from Finland, and her original spelling was "marjuwle," but when she moved to the United States, it was changed to my spelling. I did call her up because she may be the only non-family Marjule in the entire world! (laughter)

Q: Please tell our readers about your parents.

Marjule: My parents were Marjule and Edward Groeschel. My mother grew up in Bayonne, New Jersey, and my dad grew up in Jersey City, New Jersey.

Chapter 1: Marjule Drury

My mother was one of four children. My father had two brothers.

Q: Did your father travel around a bit for his work?

Marjule: Yes, my dad worked on the roadways in the beginning. He was a civil engineer, and he used to take the train out from Jersey City to go to Hackettstown, but they would always stop in Caldwell, and my dad just loved it here. He thought Caldwell was like paradise, and back in the 1940s, it probably was. He told my mother all about it, and they decided to move. A year after they moved to Caldwell, I was born.

Q: So you were the only one born here in Caldwell, New Jersey?

Marjule: My four older brothers, except one, were born in Jersey City. One was born in Berkeley Heights, then came my sister and me.

Q: So you are one of the youngest Groeschel children. How much older is your brother, Father Benedict?

Marjule: He is 13 years older than I am, and when my sister Robin was born, I was two, and my mother did not come home from the hospital for eight months. So Benedict was my primary caregiver. He'd come home from school, pick me up from the babysitter, and take care of me until my dad came home.

So he said to me, maybe four or five years ago, that if I ever feel that there's something wrong with me, blame it on him and just keep on going! (laughter)

Q: So he's your scapegoat?

Marjule: Yes! (laughter) There were four boys and then two girls. Benedict was first, and Edward, who we called Ned, was second. Gerard, who we called Gary, was third. Mark, who was two years older than I, was fourth. Then there was me and my sister Robin.

Mark passed away in 1983. He was a Type I childhood diabetic, and he died from complications. Ned passed away in November of 2008 from complications after a bad fall that he had.

Chapter 1: Marjule Drury

Q: So your oldest brother, whom you always knew as Peter and eventually became Benedict, goes into the seminary at 18 years old. Do you have any early memories of that, since you would have been only five then?

Marjule: Oh yes, I remember the day he left because my mother was extremely upset because when he entered the Capuchins, we were not allowed to see him for two years! There was no contact at all. It was like he was moving from our family to another family, and that was really hard for her. But after two years had passed, we were allowed to go visit once a month on a Sunday.

Q: And where was that?

Marjule: Up in Garrison, New York, and it was a seminary, and there wasn't anything for my sister or me to do. We were so little, but we used to sit out on the big lawn overlooking the Hudson River, and I remember sitting on his lap and combing his beard. We were fascinated with the beard he had grown.

Q: He did not have one prior to his entering?

Marjule: Oh no, but once he entered, that was the rule. They needed to have a beard. He was happy to see us, and we were happy to be there. Every time I would take a picture of him when I saw him, he was always smiling.

Q: Did you think your family knew he had a vocation in the works?

Marjule: Absolutely! Now my father was a practical person. You might even say he could be a bit cynical. He did work in New York City, and I suppose that can make you a little cynical, but my mother was very close to us all, and she knew early on about his vocation. Benedict says he knew he was going to be a priest at seven years of age, and I believe him.

Q: What did you see at an early age?

Marjule: Well, what I saw was that he spent most of his time after school up at Caldwell College and Mt. St. Dominic. He would go up there for art lessons. He loved art, and the nuns would teach him in exchange for cleaning the classrooms because it was not coed.

Chapter 1: Marjule Drury

It was strictly female, but Benedict and the Mother Superior were very much alike, and he had great respect for her.

Q: Your brother always seems to get along with many different people…

Marjule: Yes, and I remember years ago at our parish, St. Aloysius in Caldwell, there was our sexton, an elderly man named Patty Callaghan. My brother spent a lot of time at St. Aloysius, so he got to know Patty very well and was fascinated by him in his early years. Patty had been a jockey in Ireland. Patty and Benedict became good friends.

Well, Patty was trying to set up a room for himself in the basement of the church rectory where he could live, and my mother was going to give him a table and some chairs. So he came over to our house, and Benedict naturally helped him move the items.

Patty and Benedict put the chairs in the car we had, an old yellow Hudson Hornet, and then they took the table and laid it on the roof with a little rope to try and hold it on. Benedict was too young to drive. Patty obviously wasn't, but I don't think he had a license.

Q: No?

Marjule: Well, he certainly did not drive a car as well as he used to ride a horse! (laughter) So, Benedict and Patty are in the Hudson driving up Bloomfield Avenue, which is the main street in our town of Caldwell. The light turns red right in front of where the Presbyterian Church is, and Patty slams on the brakes, which results in the table sliding forward and going off the hood of the car and out into the center of the street! It was a sight as the two of them were in the street, blocking traffic, trying to get the table back up on top of the Hudson Hornet!

But you know something, despite the age difference, Patty Callaghan enjoyed my brother's company because he could see something in Benedict. Patty was a good man, but he was also a crazy Irishman. (laughter)

Q: Where did your brother go to school?

Marjule: Benedict went to Immaculate Conception high school in Montclair, and he was an excellent orator. He won tons of medals. If you walk into that school today, his name is still up on the plaque.

Unfortunately, I also went to Immaculate Conception high school, and I would hear from Sister Gertrude, "You are nothing like your brother!" (laughter)

Q: That must have been a rough comparison?

Marjule: There was no way you could even aspire to be like him. I truly believe that intelligence was just born in him.

Q: Did your brother take more after your father or mother?

Marjule: Neither! (laughter) He was different from all of us.

My mother was an extremely generous woman and worked very hard. She gave a lot of her time volunteering. Now, of course, she had six children, and in our early days, before I was born, we moved a lot because my father had different construction projects either up in New York or in New Jersey, and there was one out in Ashtabula, Ohio.

My mother would organize the wives of all the other workers, and she would make sure they never missed Holy Days or holidays and that everyone always had decent food to eat and a good place to live. She was like a Mother Superior to the other women. (laughter)

Q: Were either your mother or father avid readers?

Marjule: Well, my mother was. Every day when I came home from school, she would be sitting in her chair in the living room reading.

Q: Where did your mother work?

Marjule: She worked for a company in Livingston, New Jersey, called Burrells Press Clipping. She would have a list of clients, and she would read newspapers from across the United States and look for articles about those clients so they could track their notoriety and media coverage in different areas of the country. She worked there for many years and had a lot of friends there. So reading was her business, but it was also her pleasure. My mother loved to read mysteries.

Q: Let's go back to your father and some of his work. He did some very impressive jobs. Can you share some of the projects he worked on?

Chapter 1: Marjule Drury

Marjule: He worked on the Chrysler Building in Manhattan and then spent a lot of time working on the roadways. He got a job in New York City for Turner Construction, where he helped build Madison Square Garden and other buildings, but you know most of the buildings he built were done when I was small and unaware. He did work on the New York City tunnels but not the bridges.

Q: Tunnels like the Lincoln Tunnel, which connects New Jersey to Manhattan?

Marjule: Yes, and he also worked on Lincoln Center. That was great because when that was finished, and the ballet was preparing for opening night, everyone who worked on Lincoln Center was invited to attend their final dress rehearsal. We went and it was awesome!

My father knew New York City pretty well and probably knew it just as well 300 feet below ground, especially when they did Madison Square Garden. He would bring home the plans and spread them all over the dining room table, and he tried to explain to me what certain things were, how support beams were used, and what they did when they got down to bedrock. My father loved all of the planning and working with the architectural plans.

Q: After being ordained as a Capuchin priest for a while, Father Benedict studied and became a psychologist. Do you have any insights into how he got into that field?

Marjule: Well, I know before he went into the seminary, he spent a lot of time visiting people who lived in less fortunate areas, and he had an affinity for talking with people, helping them solve their problems, giving them advice, but also giving them tangible assistance that they needed. So it wasn't only talk.

I think Benedict always had an insight into people, which may have helped push him toward psychology. But I know when he became a psychologist, he was the first one ever to become one in his order. I don't know whose suggestion it was to go to school for that because when you are a member of an order, you take orders! I don't know how much freedom he had to make suggestions.

Chapter 1: Marjule Drury

Q: Traditionally, many sons, particularly the oldest in a family, might follow in their father's footsteps. Do you have any thoughts about your brother doing something quite different, like psychology?

Marjule: Well, I knew Benedict had a mind different than the rest of us. He was really in a world we just weren't familiar with. I don't know if he got some of his psychological thinking when he was in the seminary, but I could picture him, if he were not a priest, being a psychologist. He loved to talk to people and help them with their problems.

Q: What were your thoughts about the transition Father Benedict made when he left the Capuchins with some others and began the Franciscan Friars of the Renewal? Did you say to yourself, "Oh my! What are you doing?"

Marjule: I didn't say that, but I thought it was very exciting, and when he explained to me why he was doing it, I thought, "Of course, what else can you do?"

It was part of his personality, and the reason he became a Franciscan was to follow St. Francis of Assisi, and when the Capuchins kind of went a little to the left, that was not what he wanted and not what he felt he was responsible for doing.

So I was excited, but I was worried for him because it was all contingent on the approval of the Holy Father at the time. There was some risk involved because Benedict was not as well known then as he is today. I do remember my father was so proud that Benedict was starting a new community. He understood it and liked the work, but it was extra special because his son was getting approval from the Holy Father!

So it did surprise me at first, but then I realized, of course, he had no choice and none of the others did either. I never pictured them banding together and saying they were going to secede from the Capuchins. It wasn't like that. It was just the eight of them, and they all had the same mindset, and thank God it worked!

Q: It is amazing to see that, currently, there are more novices and seminarians in the CFRs than archdiocesan vocations in New York's St. Joseph's

Chapter 1: Marjule Drury

Seminary. Do you see this community's growth as a work of the Holy Spirit?

Marjule: Absolutely! Anytime I am with my brother, or if I see him on television when he's about to speak or to pray, he always says, "Come, Holy Spirit. Come and be with us. Guide us."

And that is how he starts everything. So I know definitely it is the Holy Spirit that has been with the community, as well as a lot of hard work. I think so many join the CFRs because they all want what Benedict wanted. They want to be as close to St. Francis of Assisi as they can. And they truly believe when Jesus said to drop everything, leave your family, and follow Him. And that you don't need anything. You will get what you need on your journey.

Q: It is certainly nice to see the young vocations coming into the Franciscan Friars of the Renewal.

Marjule: Well, during the last 20 years, the young ones who have come are so hungry for something close to God. That's why they chose the CFRs. My problem is that I know so many of them I can't remember all of their names. (laughter) So many times,

I just say, "Hi, Brother," and that generally works for me.

Q: Do you have any favorite thoughts or experiences as you have interacted with the CFRs?

Marjule: Yes, when they opened Most Blessed Sacrament in Newark, which is the friary they took over from the Dominicans, the CFRs started an associates program, so I joined. One Saturday a month, I'd go down at nine o'clock, get coffee, a bagel, or a doughnut, and then the CFRs would give out assignments; places in the friary that needed cleaning or repairs. They had all kinds of things that needed to be done inside as well as outside, like yard work. It was awesome, and I just loved going.

Q: What did you do at Most Blessed Sacrament?

Marjule: Usually, they would put me in the chapel with three other women, and we would polish everything. But one time, they sent us up to the tailor's room. One of the Brothers had been a tailor in his other life before joining the CFRs, and we walked into that room, and it was very disorganized. It really needed help.

Well, we spent the whole day up there, and when the group of us was done, it was spotless! Even the rolls of threads were wound up tight and color-coordinated.

Just walking into Most Blessed Sacrament or the kitchen at Trinity Retreat in Larchmont or anywhere my brother is, and I am around people who know me, I just get a feeling that it's going to be a good day, regardless of what is going on.

Q: You can't listen to a Father Benedict homily, teaching, conference, audio, or video tape without hearing an injection of humor. Where does that humor come from?

Marjule: Right in here. (Pointing to her chest) Right below his heart, there is a little tiny Jewish comedian. I've always said that, and I think it's from his years in Jersey City and just living in a crazy household. We probably contributed to his humor, which can be a little sarcastic and cutting.

But also, over the years, he has seen that a little bit of comedy puts people at ease and makes them more responsive and receptive to the message he is giving.

The comedy makes people like him. It cuts down the distance between him and the audience. It makes people think that he's not so stoic, strong, and loud, and filled with hell, fire, and brimstone. He enjoys talking from his heart to other people's hearts, and he likes to make them laugh.

Q: Was he always like that?

Marjule: Definitely. You know we had a picture of Benedict from when he was young, probably during his high school years, and I always laughed when I saw it because he had such a smirk on his face! (laughing) You just knew that the camera was picking up a moment when he was creating something funny to say! He can make anyone laugh.

Q: Father Benedict has written about 34 books, and he has been pumping them out for many years, sometimes a couple during a given year. What were your thoughts when you saw some of his published work?

Chapter 1: Marjule Drury

Marjule: It stunned me when he started to write. In the very beginning, when his books were printed, I was a teenager, getting close to 18 years old, and the last thing I had on my mind was the subject matter of his books.

But people started commenting to me that they had just got a new book from him, and I would see his books listed in catalogs we would receive in the mail. Eventually, when he started appearing on EWTN, his book sales really took off. Before that, he usually sold most of his books when he went out speaking, and he always brought boxes of them with him.

I knew every time he would take a plane ride, he would write. Every time he went on a long car ride, like to Washington, D.C., he would write. He writes everything in longhand, and it's worse than chicken scratch! (laughter) But he has a good soul to transcribe.

As I got older, I began to wonder how he wrote because, for me, it is very difficult. A writer needs to really organize their thoughts; you need literary strings that run through your work to make your ideas connect. I couldn't figure out how he was doing it, but I believe he could do it through the Holy Spirit.

He told me once he came across Father Solanus Casey when he was in ecstasy on the altar, and I have a feeling when Benedict writes that sometimes he gets into a place somewhere in his head and the words just flow. You know, I have seen some of his handwritten manuscripts, and there is hardly anything that is crossed out where he might have changed his mind or decided to use different words to express an idea. His writing just flows, and his ideas just pour right out of him, thanks to the Holy Spirit.

Q: Do you have a favorite book?

Marjule: I enjoy *Everday Encounters with God*. That is a good one. I know for people who have had difficult times, *Arise From Darkness* is a popular book. When my husband died, after a few months, Benedict suggested that I read it again, but because I am his sister, I never needed to read it again. I knew the book, and I was doing ok.

Q: And what about some of the audio or video tape series? Do you have any favorites from them?

Marjule: I like watching his tapes because I am more of a visual person. He did some tapes on Ireland when he went on a pilgrimage there, and I really enjoyed seeing a lot of those places.

Some people I know listen to his audio tapes in the car when they are out driving on business or commuting into New York City.

Q: Many people do not get to see Father Benedict in person, at least not on a regular basis. Many people see him on television or on tape or DVD. Obviously, you have had the opportunity to see him speak in person many times and in many different environments. Are there any special memories that you have?

Marjule: Well, I went to see him speak for three hours on Good Friday at St. Patrick's Cathedral in Manhattan. I was with a group of my friends, and we were unknown to most people there, which was good. It was really awesome to see him up there.

And then there was his 25th anniversary at Sacred Heart in Yonkers. That was an awesome day, and I remember a choir came down from Harlem, and so many priests came to be with him dressed in their finest vestments. It was a very impressive day, and I was very happy for him.

Q: Of course, so many are happy that there is a 50th anniversary for Father Benedict, particularly when we think about a few years back. It is a difficult subject but can you share some of what happened when your brother was struck by a car in Orlando back in January of 2004?

Marjule: Well, Father John Lynch had called, and I answered the phone in my kitchen. When I finally figured out what he was saying to me, I collapsed and fell to the floor. Edward, my husband, was in the living room, and he jumped up and yelled, "What's the matter? What's wrong?"

I continued to listen to Father John, and I just kept saying, "I need to come. I need to come."

And Father John was saying, "No, don't come here. He may not be here when you get here." And I couldn't believe it.

All these years and nothing had ever happened to Benedict. All of the traveling around the world, and then all he was doing was crossing the street at an airport!

So I called everyone in my family, and I called my friends in the Rosary Society. I called my boss because we have a prayer group in our company all over the country. And we just prayed and prayed and prayed.

After a week, Benedict was still with us. So I packed my bags and went down to Orlando because I couldn't wait any longer. When I got there, Father John actually explained to me that Benedict had died and had no vital signs for 27 minutes. He was telling me all this in the room in front of Benedict, who was in bed in an induced coma because of the horrendous pain.

And as Father John was explaining all that happened, I just looked at Benedict and thought, "Wow, why are you still here?"

And as time went on and he went home and got stronger and stronger, it became evident why he was still here. He had more work that needed to be done.

From February to October of that year, I would spend every Saturday up at Trinity Retreat or at Burke Rehabilitation Center in New Rochelle with him. And you know that is when I really became very close to him. I always considered him as my brother, and I remember little snippets of him when I was young, but now I was able to interact with him as two adults. Yes, still brother and sister, but I was in a position where I could help him. He always was the one helping everyone else. Now it was time for him to receive. And I never planned anything for Saturdays. It was always a time to be with him.

Q: What did you think when he received something like 50,000 emails from around the world?

Marjule: Well, I wasn't surprised. One of the most well-known religious people in my lifetime was Mother Teresa. She's known everywhere and respected by everyone. Even those who don't like her respect her. And Benedict was friends with Mother Teresa for 30 years. So through his connections with her, a lot of people got to know him. And with the technology of email, it's so easy to get one's immediate feelings out, so it was not surprising so many people wrote.

Of course, the Friars took care of all that, and they did print out and highlighted a number of them. Benedict did read an awful lot of them.

I was pleased with the show of support, but at the same time, I was taken back because all of that overwhelming response encircles him. It's not that I can't fit in with the multitude of people, but I really don't want to. I'm in a different place than where Benedict is.

Q: You mentioned Mother Teresa. Did you ever get the chance to meet her?

Marjule: No, I never did, but my children did get the opportunity at a church in Newark. Mother Teresa was very kind to them. She put her hand on my daughter's cheek and patted my son's head, and I thought that was quite wonderful.

It's a funny thing with me and famous people in the Church. I love that they're there. I love what they do, for the most part. I love that they help people and encourage people to help others. But I never really have a need to meet them. (laughter)

Q: How about Cardinal Cooke?

Marjule: I was very impressed with Cardinal Cooke. He had a very special connection with Benedict.

When my dad died, we had the funeral here in Caldwell, and Cardinal Cooke came for the Mass. My brother did the Mass, and the cardinal did get up to speak. After it was over, everyone was outside in front of the church, and there was Cardinal Cooke, who at the time was dying, but was as nice as could be.

The fact he put himself through that showed me a lot. Cardinal Cooke was always concerned with others, and it was a privilege to meet him.

Q: When you think about your brother reaching his 50th Golden Anniversary as a priest, what are some of your thoughts and feelings?

Marjule: Well, he was never one to quit anything, even when things got hard. I knew when I saw him for the first time in that brown robe as a Capuchin that that was it. I said to myself, "This is my brother, and this is what he's going to be for his entire life."

And I was happy that he became a priest and did not remain a Brother because I felt he had too much to offer. And as the years went on, I knew he was trapped as a Capuchin. Not unwillingly trapped, but

I knew he would never leave the priesthood. He was tied to God, and he was born to be a priest.

Q: Do you think about his legacy? What people will remember him for?

Marjule: Well, the way the general public will remember him is that they will be grateful for him. I believe the people he touched, before and during his priesthood, will be very grateful to him and for him. He made them feel good no matter how rotten they felt about themselves. He stressed God's mercy so that they knew they were loved, and I think that gave many people solace.

Within the Catholic Church and within the religious community, I think Benedict had a great deal of influence. He gave them very helpful instruction. He was able to be with them in confidence, take their struggles and help untwist them and get their life back on track, with the Holy Spirit's help, of course.

He was able to get this Church through one of the worst times in the last 100 years, and he defends the Church completely. But he always says to me and to others, "The Church to me is Jesus Christ, and I follow Jesus Christ. The people within the Church make mistakes and sometimes sin horrendously, but if you concentrate on the Divine, on Christ, you can't go wrong."

The priests who did what they did are human beings and have tremendous psychological problems. Benedict understands those problems, and he can forgive those problems. However, many times he cannot change those problems or rehabilitate the person, but that's what he tries to do.

Q: Was the priest sex scandal the most challenging time for Father Benedict?

Marjule: I think only one time did my brother ever say to me how hurt he was, and that was when one of the kids at Children's Village committed suicide. That took a tremendous toll on him, not to the point he ever thought of giving up, but I think it caused him to think harder, work harder, and look at ways to prevent people with great difficulties from choosing something like suicide.

Q: Had you ever visited Father Benedict at Children's Village in Dobbs Ferry, New York?

Chapter 1: Marjule Drury

Marjule: Yes.

Q: And what was your impression?

Marjule: It was great, and I loved the kids there. I would walk around the grounds where they had a duck and a dog, and I remember the chapel was really beautiful. It was heart-warming to see all the kids in chapel. As troubled as they were, they were there, and they were trying.

Children's Village was my first glimpse of how many children didn't have families. I had no clue that so many children got into trouble.

Q: Father Benedict has a long-standing relationship with Good Counsel and is our co-founder. How did you get involved in helping the organization?

Marjule: Through my brother. I did meet Chris Bell and his wife, along with a few of their children. I did work on a fundraiser for Good Counsel at St. Thomas More Church in Fairfield, New Jersey. We needed a speaker, and of course, Benedict was invited to come.

Q: Do you think it was natural for Father Benedict to become Good Counsel's chairman of the board of directors?

Marjule: Yes, because if you follow Jesus Christ, as Benedict does, you know that abortion is murder. There is no other word for it.

There was an old black woman in New York who was very fond of Benedict. She had five small granddaughters that she was caring for. Well, this grandmother died, and in her will she asked if Benedict would be their spiritual guide, and you know, every year they still get together. This goes back many years because the girls are now all adults and grown.

But this is all part of Benedict's character. He has always felt children are the heart of the Church. They are the lifeblood. What would we do without children? And to see people killing their children is just so abhorrent and against any sort of natural law, so it did not surprise me when I saw him get involved with Good Counsel homes.

Chapter 2

Christopher Bell

Christopher Bell is the President and Co-founder of Good Counsel homes, which cares for homeless pregnant mothers and their children. Chris co-founded Good Counsel, Inc., with Father Benedict Groeschel in Hoboken, New Jersey, in 1985.

Q: It is amazing how many stories different people have about how they first met Father Benedict. Everyone seems to have vivid memories of their first encounter. Can you please share your first meeting?

Chris: I was living and working in a crisis center in the Times Square section of New York City. I was living in a lay prayer community helping homeless, runaway, and abandoned teenagers, and it was the worst day I spent doing that.

Early in the morning, when I first went down to the center, I saw a young man who I knew was not supposed to be inside. He was getting "walk-in" services, but he wasn't supposed to be in the middle of the living room, so I went up to him and said, "You know you're not supposed to be here."

His response was to take a swing at me. He missed, but it created a bit of a mini-riot. Other counselors came in and had to quell the disturbance, and this young man was tackled. It was just a terrible morning because the result of everything was he had to be rejected from services for a period of time, and I felt bad because that day he was going to begin a job program, and he had short-circuited this great opportunity to better himself.

Q: So after that emotionally charged scene, what then developed?

Chris: Well, every evening at 5:30 pm, we had Mass in the community chapel right off 8th Avenue in what was known as the Minnesota strip. Most of the visiting priests who came to us would begin by saying, "What a wonderful, beautiful work you are doing!"

And I sat back on this particular evening seeing there was a visiting priest, not knowing anything else at all about Father Benedict, and I said to myself, "If this priest says anything about how great we are, I'm going to puke!"

I did sit back, and he began to talk and said, "Many people think of St. John Bosco surrounded by these cherubic faces, helping these wonderful, beautiful street kids. That's not true at all! They were tough kids. They were difficult kids. They were like your kids!" And I realized instantly that he understood, maybe better than anybody, that these kids were really different and our work wasn't easy.

And then after Mass, he talked to us about the spiritual life, which I had never before heard about from a Catholic perspective. So Father Benedict said to us, "I preach regularly at a neighborhood parish; maybe you can stop in and see me. I also have a retreat house; maybe you can all come up for a day of recollection or weekend."

Q: So you took him up on his offer?

Chris: Yes, I went to go to his talks at a midtown Manhattan parish, and I went to visit him and talked a lot, and we did become very close. By the next year, I asked if he would become my spiritual director, and he did.

Q: What year are you talking about?

Chris: I met Father Benedict sometime in the winter of 1980.

Q: So it is coming up on 30 years that you have known him. Has Father Benedict changed much during these last 30 years?

Chris: In some ways he's become wiser, if that is possible, but essentially he has always had a very close communion with Our Lord. He certainly is a son of St. Augustine as much as he is a son of St. Francis of Assisi.

I think his ability to deal with people grows greater, if that is possible. From the beginning, he has always had the keenest ability to evaluate, to read someone, to know something about them very deep inside, both spiritually and psychologically. He is very sensitive and very humble because, with all he knows and all he does and all that he could brag about himself, he never does. In fact, he loathes to think that anyone would give him any adulation.

Q: Of course, a lot of your involvement with Father Benedict has centered on Good Counsel homes. Can you share a little about how you approached him to be involved with this outreach?

Chris: While working in Times Square, I saw a large number of pregnant teens and women who were looking for help, and no one was able to give them the assistance they really needed. When I told Father

Benedict about this problem, I expected him to inform me who was really taking up the slack and where I should go, but I discovered no one really was addressing the issue and needs of homeless pregnant mothers and their children. When I suggested to him that I begin working in this area, because I thought that's what God was asking me to do, he said, "I'll help you." Father Benedict told me, "If you want to do this, I'll do whatever I can to help."

Now, I didn't realize right then how vitally important his help, his support, and his name were. But you know, even at that time in 1984 when I left Times Square to start Good Counsel, almost every priest in the Greater New York metropolitan area knew him! It wasn't because he was on television or that he had done several dozen videos and audio tape series that were being circulated around. It was because he was a nationally recognized retreat master and lecturer, and most of the priests had been taught by him in the seminary.

Q: And his support came because he had done similar work before?

Chapter 2: Christopher Bell

Chris: I think Father Benedict recognized that what I was looking to do was God's call, and as strange as it sounds, for two guys to reach out and help mothers and babies, it was something he supported. Traditionally, it was religious orders of women or single women who would help other women, and the priests and religious brothers would help homeless boys. Father Benedict had already started a home for young men called St. Francis Home in Green Point, Brooklyn, and he had been running that maybe two decades by the time I met him. His support opened up doors and relieved a lot of potential fears of religious and chanceries both in New York and New Jersey.

Q: What was Father Benedict's response when you asked him to be chairman of Good Counsel's Board of Directors?

Chris: When we first began helping homeless mothers and children, we didn't have a corporation. It was just under the egress of the Church, and after a while, many of our supporters said to me that we needed to incorporate. Father Benedict said, "We need to keep this simple. Small is beautiful." There wasn't any coaxing or cajoling. I think it was a natural understanding that we needed a board, and when I suggested that he should chair, he did not hesitate at all in saying, "Of course, I'll help." And that is how Father Benedict is. He would do anything to help.

He does not take a title, whether Director of the Office of Spiritual Development for the Archdiocese of New York or Servant for the Franciscan Friars of the Renewal, as a reflection of himself. It is a responsibility and a duty that he fulfills to the best of his abilities, knowing that God gives him the strength and the wisdom which allows him to do whatever good he can.

Q: Can you share some reflections on how it has been seeing Father Benedict as the chairman of Good Counsel's board?

Chris: It is very humbling to watch him. It makes me realize, even in his capacity as chairman, he never bangs the gavel. Not that we have one (laughter). He never commands what needs to be done. He always listens to whatever dialogue or argumentation that is presented and just offers his perspective. Do you know, in the vast majority of cases, everyone on the board will wait to see what Father Benedict will say? And when Father Benedict speaks, people listen.

His advice has proven itself time after time. There were instances when our finances have been down, or we were facing a bit of difficulty, but an opportunity for expansion came about, which on a surface level, appeared to be risky. If Father Benedict saw that the opportunity appeared to be given from God, he would wholeheartedly support the effort and convince others that it was the right thing to do. And the reverse is true. He has looked at Good Counsel plans that, on a surface level, appeared to be fine, but he felt something just was not right, including one very dramatic case, and he helped us avoid some difficulties. He has an ability to pick up some things that the rest of us miss.

Q: Next year, Good Counsel turns 25 years old. One of the things that separate the homes from a typical shelter is "Life Skills" programs that are taught by the staff and your volunteers inside of the residences. Can you describe a little about these programs?

Chris: We have five official Life Skill programs. Health, which is usually taught by a staff member, has a great syllabus and covers many areas including healthy eating, a healthy lifestyle, the health of one's child, and sexual integrity.

We have a whole section on chastity, which is not talked a whole lot about outside of our circles. Chastity not only means living one's life and abstaining from sex before marriage, but especially today, you need to talk about faithfulness within marriage.

Another Life Skill program we have is Child Growth and Development. It helps our mothers look for various milestones in their child's growth and ways to stimulate their development. What is really good about this program is that mothers can utilize the information while they are with us and when they leave and are in their own apartment.

We also have a Nutrition Program that covers everything from eating well, cooking well, and learning to shop healthy and economically. And there is a Personal Finance Program as well as a Parenting Life Skill program.

Q: Many people know that you married a rather famous woman in the pro-life movement. Your wife,

Chapter 2: Christopher Bell

formerly known as Joan Andrews, wrote in one of her books that she did not think she would ever marry, but then you came along! Can you share a little bit about how you met Joan, and did Father Benedict witness your marriage?

Chris: Well, as I began listening to the stories of the moms inside our Good Counsel homes, I knew I needed to be more involved in the pro-life movement, and I regularly began going to the March for Life in Washington, D.C., and other pro-life events. I remember at a New Jersey Right to Life conference, I met Susan Brindle, who is Joan's sister, and she was handing out fliers that described Joan's prison term in Florida.

Joan was in prison with a horribly unjust sentence of five years for peacefully, prayerfully, and non-violently trying to stop an abortion. She would just go into the abortion mill and just sit down. In those days, it created a great deal of havoc, so they would usually close down the mill for the day at least.

Well, Joan was arrested, and because it was the first rescue to stop an abortion in Florida, the judge was irate when Joan refused to cooperate by promising never to return to the abortion mill again. So, in figurative terms, the judge threw the book at Joan.

Q: So, did you visit Joan in prison?

Chris: When I met Susan, Joan's sister, she asked me if I would like to make a visit, and I was happy to learn that Joan had been extradited up to Delaware. I asked Susan what Joan might like me to bring: magazines, religious articles, pamphlets, and a cake with a file in it! (laughter) And Susan told me that Joan did not get an opportunity to receive Communion very often, so I told her that, being a Eucharistic Minister, I would be happy to bring Joan the Blessed Sacrament.

Well, unfortunately, I did not have a pix, which is the little gold case that one carried the Body of Christ in, but the pastor where I was staying allowed me to take Our Lord in an Altar cloth, which was great because the pix would have set off the metal detector at the prison, and they may have confiscated it!

So I met Joan in a small room with about a dozen other prisoners and their guests, and there were two guards at the front of the room. When I told Joan that I had the Blessed Sacrament with me and asked if she would like to receive it, she said, "That's wonderful, but if the guards see you give me anything, they may think it's drugs, and then they might arrest you!"

And I said, "Thank you!"

Then she said, "Wait until everyone gets up at the end of our visit. When they get up, I will kneel down and receive."

And I thought to myself, "Of course! The guards won't notice somebody kneeling down on the floor and me giving her something!" (laughter)

But I let that go and we started to talk, and I learned she had been praying with the women in prison, and it was like a ministry for her. I saw she was willing to suffer for the Lord without any complaints at all, and I was deeply moved.

Q: And as you left the visiting room?

Chris: Miraculously, at the end, as everyone got up to leave, she knelt down and received Our Lord, and I wasn't arrested! I think our guardian angels protected us!

And as I drove back from that visit, I thought if I were ever to get married it would be to Joan, yet I didn't think it was possible, not only because of her jail time, but because both of our ministries were so different and so intense.

Q: But it did happen...

Chris: Well, six months after my visit, Joan was finally released from jail, but she would travel around the country and talk to groups about the rescue movement. And when she would be around New York, I would show up at an event and tap her on the shoulder and say, "Hi, you probably don't remember me. I'm Chris Bell, and we met in a Delaware prison!" She would always say that she remembered me, but I thought she was just being polite.

You know, time went on, and in truth, it was a year after we were married that I found out that I was really set up by Joan's sister Susan. Joan and I were speaking to a couple of hundred high school students about how we met, and she told everyone, including me, "In my jail cell, I had a picture of the Sacred Heart, a picture of the Immaculate Heart of Mary, and a picture of Chris!"

Chapter 2: Christopher Bell

Q: So you were in good company...

Chris: Yes, and I do realize that even though I was set up because Susan had given Joan the picture of me, there was also God's grace.

Q: And Father Benedict did witness your wedding. But where was it?

Chris: We did look at many churches because Joan was unaffiliated with a parish, and so was I, even though I had been living in Hoboken for about six years.

Q: Primarily because you were on the road traveling to churches on many Sundays speaking for Good Counsel?

Chris: Yes, and after asking Father Benedict to witness the marriage, we just figured that it would probably be best to go to St. Crispin's Chapel in the South Bronx. That is where the Franciscan Friars of the Renewal began, and Joan did fall in love with the place. We did separately spend the night before our wedding in the South Bronx at the Friary, but that morning we both got up early to spend some quiet prayer time at the Corpus Christi Monastery, where the Dominican Sisters have a cloister. It was just a few miles away from the Friars. I won't say that we were caught up in the spirit, but we certainly prayed a great deal, and on our way back to St. Crispin's, we did get lost. Most people think of either a bride or a groom being late for their wedding, but we were together, and both of us were late for our wedding. (laughter)

Q: So Father Benedict was there waiting for you at the altar? Did he say something like, "Did you kids decide to elope?"

Chris: Well, let me put it this way, he was not very happy. But being late together is how our marriage began, and thanks be to God, almost eleven months to the day afterward, Mary Louise, our first child, was born.

Q: You have been doing adoption outreach unofficially for a while, and it is interesting to note that you and Joan do have a number of adopted children.

Chris: Yes, about two and a half years after Mary Louise was born, we did adopt our first son, Emiliano, who was born in Mexico, and then we adopted a child, Philomena, who was born in Pennsylvania, but her mother was from the Caribbean and her father was from Africa.

Q: And you made a couple of trips to Russia?

Chris: Yes, we went back and forth to Russia a couple of times and adopted four beautiful children, and they have special needs, as does Emiliano, but sometimes I think I have more special needs than they do! (laughter)

Chapter 3

Dr. Ann Marie Wallace

Ann Marie Wallace, Ph.D., served as Director of the Archdiocese of New York's Center for Spiritual Development, which provides ongoing spiritual formation for adult Christians. Dr. Wallace worked with Father Benedict Groeschel for many years and arranged many pilgrimages, retreats, and spirituality programs with him.

Q: Let's start by asking what is the difference between the Archdiocese of New York's Center for Spiritual Development and the Office for Spiritual Development?

Ann: The Center for Spiritual Development is dedicated to lay people and all of the programs we have happen out in the community. The Office for Spiritual Development is run by Father Benedict and is for the needs of the clergy. Both of our programs deal with much of the same material, but the Office for Spiritual Development addresses issues from the perspective of living a religious vocation. Priests come from all over the country to see Father Benedict and often see him in an office setting or on retreat.

Q: Like many people, you have had an interesting journey to where you are today. How did you get to be Director of the Center for Spiritual Development?

Ann: Well, I went to school at Marymount Manhattan College on 71st. Street in New York and then went to Fordham University for my Masters. I chose my Masters program because I wanted to pursue things with an English degree, but when I started working at a Junior High School, I realized that an English Degree was not going to do a great deal for the needs of the students or for myself.

Subsequently, I was talking with one of the staff, an assistant counselor, who told me they would be studying at Fordham, and I asked what they would be majoring in. They told me counseling, and so I said, "Where do I sign up?"

Q: Sounds like one of those divinely inspired conversations...

Ann: That's what led me to work on my doctorate in counseling, and it's been very helpful, especially in my work in spiritual direction and one of the classes I taught in Father Benedict's program on Skills of Spiritual Direction.

Q: And that was before you got involved with the Center?

Ann: Yes, at that point, I was teaching at Fairfield University in Connecticut, and I was Division Director of the Counseling program, so I was able to work in both places. I also was invited to go over to St. Joseph's Seminary in Yonkers, New York. The priests there were learning what Father Benedict was doing in the area of spiritual development, and I was invited in and subsequently got involved with the Archdiocese of New York's Catechetical Institute Program, where we were able to combine psychology with spiritual development.

Q: It's an important point that shouldn't be passed over quickly. Not many people were doing that. How did you make the connection between counseling and spiritual development? Was it something you stumbled into, or was it something already inside you?

Ann: I guess it was around 1964 when I became Principal of St. Paul the Apostle School in Yonkers. I was the first layperson in that role. It was wonderful, but I knew it was not something I was called to do. As things turned out, the school did close, and I realized that I needed to do something else and that kind of began the process of finding out where I belonged.

Chapter 3: Dr. Ann Marie Wallace

Q: But from there you went on to Fairfield University. What did you teach there?

Ann: I was teaching Adult Psychology which was in the Adult Counseling Program. I thought I would stay two years, but I kept coming back again and again, and before you knew it, I was there for ten years! And after ten years, I received a message from Father Benedict, who wanted to talk to me. He asked me if I would be interested in taking a job, and it was just the kind of spiritual thing I wanted to get into.

Q: Because it was combining spirituality and psychology?

Ann: Yes. Spirituality takes place in your life as you live it, and the area of Adult Psychology is very compatible with it.

Q: When you think of spirituality and psychology; are there any psychologists who you admire or have read that you think did a really nice job of blending these two studies?

Ann: Well, I have read a great deal, and it is hard to name anyone with the exception of Father Benedict.

Q: How did you find Carl Jung?

Ann: Jung, I found helpful, but he is limited. He doesn't discuss everything. I found Jung helpful in teaching about sin and the difficulties people encounter. His understanding of the dynamic of the person is very good. What is interesting to me is that we can find God in every stage of life. All of our lives change, sometimes very dramatically, but regardless of what happens, physically or psychologically, we can find God. He is always present.

Q: So let's go ahead to your becoming Director of the Center for Spiritual Development. How much autonomy did you have to do the things you wanted to do? How much rope did Father Benedict give you?

Ann: There was no rope. (laughter) It's true. He told me to run the Center, and I did. If I had a question or if there was a problem, we would discuss things, but he trusted me and believed I knew what the Church teaches and so we got along splendidly.

Chapter 3: Dr. Ann Marie Wallace 63

Q: Obviously, Father Benedict knew you before you were hired as the Center's director, so the trust issue was already in place?

Ann: Well, I had previously taken his two-year course in the spiritual growth process. That course was filled with mostly priests and religious, so I stood out as one of the few lay people there. It was a wonderful course, and as it ended, he asked me if I would teach the skills section of the spirituality program.

Q: The Center for Spiritual Development was already established when you got there, right?

Ann: Yes, it was started in 1979 by Father Bruce Nieli, a Paulist Father, who is a very good friend of Father Benedict. Cardinal Cooke had asked Father Benedict to establish a Center, and that's why Father Nieli was brought in.

Q: During your first year, Father Benedict was the main speaker, but he has been a part of the annual spirituality convocation almost every year, right?

Ann: Well, of course. He has been to every one of them except one, and that was because he was in the hospital following his near-fatal accident in Orlando. I should also mention that Father Benedict, through his many resources and connections, was able to help the convocation by personally inviting many excellent featured speakers, including many people who we had no prior contact with.

Q: Over the years, you put together some very good programs featuring people like Scott Hahn, Father Michael Scanlon from Steubenville, Father Mitch Pacwa from EWTN, and Marcus Grodi from The Coming Home Network.

Ann: And, please God, it will continue.

Q: The Center for Spiritual Development has reached out to many people, not just those living in the immediate New York City area. How far did your programs and courses reach?

Ann: Early on in the Center's history, we were in five places, and that's where Father Benedict was giving the two-year course on The Spiritual Journey. We continued to support that over a number of years, but then the numbers began to drop, and we began to look at what other things we could do. We began to develop a series of one-day programs and small retreats that have kept us busy.

Q: What is the biggest challenge the laity has with spirituality?

Ann: Well, there are probably many things, but at the root is that many are not seeing or recognizing the sacredness of attending Mass. My own parish, which is not that large, has had a steady reduction of people attending, and it is alarming because they don't know the treasures they're missing.

Q: Please talk a little about some pilgrimages and the trips your Center put together. How did that start?

Ann: Frank Brown was a local gentleman who put trips together, but not necessarily pilgrimages. He called Father Benedict and asked if he would be interested in leading a trip for priests. Well, Father Benedict contacted me and said that he didn't think the trip would get many clergy, but what about people from the Center? All I said was, "Let's find out."

We ended up with 100 people signing up and filling two tour buses in the Holy Land.

Q: That's a great place to start, going to the Holy Land with Father Benedict...

Ann: He was our leader and celebrated Mass every day in the places we visited. He had a wonderful background, history, and very inspiring stories to share from each place we traveled. All of the pilgrimages were an opportunity for all of us to get more in touch with the reality of God and for us to grow closer to God.

Q: Do you have a personal favorite trip or pilgrimage that you made with Father Benedict?

Ann: The Holy Land. It is just such a special place, and to be on the same ground where Christ walked and to stand on the shore of the Sea of Galilee takes your breath away. I remember getting up early one morning when we were at the Mount of Beatitudes, and I saw the sun coming up and it was a deep red glow. I just kept thinking that's exactly how Jesus saw

Chapter 3: Dr. Ann Marie Wallace

it and talked about it once. The Holy Land is tremendous, and, of course, Father Benedict made it even better.

Q: Were there any other trips that were meaningful?

Ann: We did go to Rome during the Holy Year. We went to Lourdes three times, but each time was different because we would cover other areas of France each time we went, seeing different shrines throughout the region. We also went to Spain.

Q: How has Father Benedict been received by the people in the Center?

Ann: He is very much loved and admired. He has opened up aspects of the spiritual journey that maybe they haven't thought of. Whenever people see that Father Benedict is involved and will be speaking, the number of people attending increases.

Q: Do you have a personal favorite Father Benedict book?

Ann: Well, I think the first book he gave me, *Spiritual Passages*, had the biggest impact on me. Whenever I had a question about something, I'd go to it and find an answer. I loved the book, and it's been with me the longest and has the most meaning to me. Additionally, *Stumbling Blocks or Stepping Stones: Spiritual Answers to Psychological Questions* is a book that I know has assisted many people. More recently, *Everyday Encounters with God* is also a book that I especially like.

Q: Switching gears, but staying on the topic of Father Benedict's books, a number of years ago, he wrote *Courage to Be Chaste*, which is a book that delves into an area not many Catholic books do. It addresses those who are struggling with homosexual tendencies and looks at the struggle to be chaste as a single person. In your work at the center, is this a subject that has been addressed in any of your programs?

Ann: We haven't gotten into that subject because I guess we made the assumption that the people who come to our events know the teaching of the Church. Obviously, problems with sexuality are there for those who are homosexual and heterosexual. I think some of the problems occur when we lose the value and sacredness of each other's bodies. We forget that the marital relationship is so special, and it is sacred and needs to be treated as such.

Q: It's a tough question, but do you think we are doing enough as a church to help those who are struggling with homosexual tendencies and who may feel alienated?

Ann: Well, feelings are important because they tell us what is going on inside a person. It is possible that there are some who don't know the teaching of the Church on areas of human sexuality who would come to a realization later in life. Certainly, Confession is something I would recommend, and that could help someone feel more connected. But a person may need to hear consoling words from the outside or talk through things to get to a better emotional place.

Q: It may be opening a can of worms with this topic, but Father Benedict does address this in *Courage to Be Chaste*... We do live in a culture

where there are more and more loud homosexual groups, some of them militaristic in their approach, pushing for things like same-sex marriage, and yet, at the same time, many of these individuals are fighting inner turmoil. Some of these people are Catholics having been Baptized and Confirmed. Do you have any thoughts on how to approach such souls?

Ann: Well, you need to ask the question, what is causing their inner turmoil? Why are they feeling uneasy? Deep down, when they discover what God truly wants for them, they will need to make a decision to stop acting on their behavioral tendencies. You know many people are unaware that Father Benedict has been involved and assisted a group called Courage.

Q: Yes, founded by Father John Harvey back in 1980. They are a Catholic group that ministers to homosexuals trying to live a chaste life.

Ann: That's right, and Father Benedict has done Courage retreats for men struggling with same-sex attraction. Also, there is another group called Encourage which reaches out to the parents of those struggling in this area.

Chapter 3: Dr. Ann Marie Wallace

Q: Moving from the area of books to television, Americans, generally speaking, are addicted to television. Some say that it has had a negative effect on our culture in terms of its spirituality. What was your impression when Father Benedict started hosting a weekly television show on EWTN (Eternal Word Television Network)?

Ann: I thought it was wonderful, and the thing that really showed how much of an impact Father Benedict has made on people is that after his accident, more than 50,000 emails were sent wishing him well and saying they were praying for him. And these emails were not just from Catholics! People writing in were Jehovah's Witnesses, Jews, and atheists. Can you imagine an atheist saying they are praying for you? Quite a remarkable thing, isn't it? The outpouring of love was from all over, and I know one person wrote in from Antarctica.

Q: Weren't you a little surprised that Father Benedict, as busy as he is, would have a weekly live show?

Ann: I think he was on a few weeks before I knew about it. I knew he had been on the network as a guest or hosting a taped series, but it was surprising that he would do a weekly live show. I do think that as people channel surf, they do discover him by accident and are blessed. Father Benedict speaks directly to people in their own language, so people are drawn in. It's very powerful when people are met at their own level and are not spoken down to.

Q: Speaking of speaking...Prayer is a way for us to speak to God. Do you see Father Benedict as a powerful prayer?

Ann: Yes, I do. I see someone who is very much in touch with God. Prayer is communion with God. Sometimes, prayer can be wordy. Sometimes, it's just sitting in the presence of God and saying, "Here I am Lord!" That's when you can allow God's grace to come into you. I think the fact Father Benedict has accomplished so much is a fruit of his prayer life. We know human intelligence only goes so far, and many times I think he gets inspiration just from listening during his prayer time. I know there are many times when he has needed to make choices to do one thing or another, and many of the good choices have come because he was listening at prayer.

Q: Which ironically is the title of one of his books! Finally, how do you think Father Benedict will be remembered?

Ann: They will remember him for what he has done for them. Father Bruce Nieli just called me yesterday, and we both have known Father Benedict for many years. As we spoke on the phone, Father Nieli told me a number of moments in his life when he was greatly assisted by Father Benedict. It wasn't like here's a problem; help me solve it. These were life-changing moments in which Father Benedict offered tremendous spiritual insight. I think Father Benedict helps people look at spirituality in a new way. He shows us interesting ways to see the faith and the Church's teachings. His words just don't pass through your ears. The words resonate in your heart and in your soul.

Chapter 4
Fr. John W. Lynch

Father John W. Lynch has been a close friend of Father Benedict Groeschel for many years and a founding member of the Franciscan Friars of the Renewal. An artist, Father John has created artwork for a number of Father Benedict's published books. Father John is a priest in the Archdiocese of New York and is the pastor of Saint Augustine's Parish in Highland, New York.

Q: Let's start at the beginning and tell me how it came about that you first met him?

Father John: The first time I saw Father Benedict was when I was invited to join a Catholic young adult group called Salt of the Earth at St. Columba Church in Hopewell Junction, New York, and as a group of young singles, at the time I was only 17, we went to visit Father Benedict in Maryknoll in Ossining, New York, to listen to his First Friday conference. Of course, he was wonderful, and it was exactly what we were trying to address in our lives, which was our faith in Jesus Christ in the orthodox fashion.

Q: How did Father Benedict relate to the young adults?

Father John: He was very good with us. He made us laugh. He made us cry, and he made things interesting so that we could be faithful followers going to see him every First Friday.

Q: Was he a Capuchin at that point?

Father John: Yes, he was a Capuchin. From that encounter with our group, he was impressed. I met him

Chapter 4: Fr. John W. Lynch

on the grounds, and he invited me to become his driver and to bring him to different places. But I needed to tell him I did not have a license or even a driver's permit, and so he told me, "Get your permit right away!" Which I did, and before you knew it, I was drawn into his fascinating world. I began driving him all over the place as his brand-new driver, and our friendship began.

Q: And how did your friendship grow from there?

Father John: Well, from there it became evident to him that I had a vocation, and I began to think so, too. So it was logical for him to help me find that vocation. My first step was my college degree, and he recommended I go to Iona College to study Psychology, which I was interested in, and Philosophy, which was necessary for the priesthood. Father Benedict taught at Iona in the Pastoral Counseling Division, and he backed everything up by saying I could live at Trinity Retreat House, and I could work there as staff, thus avoiding the painful process of living in a college dorm, which even then, I was not inclined to put up with.

Q: So Father Benedict was really taking you under his wing.

Father John: Yes, and I went to Iona College and loved it. I lived at Trinity and worked hard, and before I knew it, I became his secretary/office worker. I really had so many roles. I was a sacristan as well, and it was all good because I was able to assist Father Benedict and make his life a little easier.

Q: Did he recognize something in you first, or did you both know at the same time that you had a religious vocation? It must have been great to have him help you in such a supportive way.

Father John: Well, at 17, I was very dazzled by his intelligence and his celebrity. I mean even then, during the early days, he was pretty well known, long before EWTN and his television appearances.

Q: Doing his retreats, videos...

Father John: Yes, and that he took an interest in our young adult group. We, as a group, were quite impressed that he even knew that we existed. We were a group of teenagers and young adults going to listen to him, and he was intrigued.

We were there to learn about our faith, so what pulled us in was that he invited us to go on a retreat with him, not the other way around. In fact, none of us would have ever had the nerve to ask him, but he wanted to give us a private retreat. It is funny to remember when I phoned Trinity Retreat in Larchmont to make arrangements. I spoke with Karen Killilea, the very famous secretary there, and after listening very patiently, she asked me, "Okay, you are telling me that Father Benedict asked you if he could give you a retreat? It usually doesn't work that way."

I told her that I understood but that he did ask us to make arrangements. So Karen said, "Okay, so what year are you referring to?" And I said, "This year, perhaps in June," which was just two months away.

Karen then replied, "Excuse me, but Father Benedict's speaking schedule is booked up for the next five years, so I think you need to re-think this and when you do, call me back."

Well, we did call back and spoke to Father Benedict, and let's just say he really wanted to see us because we did not have to wait five years for a retreat, and that's really how I got the time to get to know him.

Q: Did you know Father Benedict long before he left the Capuchins and began the Franciscan Friars of the Renewal?

Father John: Well, the new community of CFRs started in 1987. You may not know, but I was a Capuchin with him after I graduated from Iona College in 1985. I was ready for the commitment, and I was ready to say yes to this vocation within the context of the Capuchins because all the mentors I knew just happened to be Capuchin Franciscans, so why not? I joined them as a Capuchin and was very happy.

Unfortunately, what happened was I had been sick for some time with a very severe hyperthyroid, which at that point was really beginning to rage in my body. I was aware that something was wrong, but I wasn't talking about it. I was losing weight dramatically, and I was generally sick but able to keep up with my studies and my duties.

It was a nice lifestyle of prayer, study, and work. It was balanced, and I did well despite everything else that was going on internally.

Chapter 4: Fr. John W. Lynch

Q: So you were a Capuchin during this famous transitional time that Father Benedict was going through?

Father John: Yes, what happened was Father Benedict and a few of the Friars invited me to go with them to start the new community of CFRs. Now you have to keep in mind I was happy where I was with the Capuchins. I had no issues. They, of course, did, which I won't go into, but as far as my story, I was content to stay where I was.

Q: But you were faced with a decision of whether to stay or whether to go and try something new which did not have official approval from the Church.

Father John: I certainly was challenged in my vocation of what I should do. Why would I leave the Capuchins? But I prayed about it, and I realized that all of my mentors – everyone who had impressed me and motivated me to become a Capuchin in the first place – were now leaving!

Everyone, bar none, was inviting me to come with them, so I thought, I guess I could go either way.

So, I reasoned to go with those who had drawn me in the first place.

Q: So, in your case, it wasn't a dramatic transition leaving the Capuchins. It went okay.

Father John: It was a little confusing at the time, but there was no drama. I wasn't doing something horrible or discouraging. I really went on faith and prayer. The Lord led me there, but the people I knew were leaving, and they invited me to go with them, which was an honor. I figured I might as well take a leap of faith and go with them.

Q: So we are now talking about 1987?

Father John: Yes, and I was doing well with the CFRs, too, and I certainly enjoyed the community life. I admired what they were trying to accomplish in a very orthodox, strict observance of the Franciscan charism. But the old bugaboo was still there; my health.

While I was with the Franciscan Friars of the Renewal, we were certainly graced and helped by Cardinal O'Connor, the former Archbishop of New

York. Father Benedict has stated many times if it had not been for Cardinal O'Connor, there would be no CFRs because, in essence, he was our founder.

Q: Because he helped get acceptance from the Church in Rome?

Father John: He provided encouragement and prayerful support. He was a true brother in this approval process because, as Father Benedict has said with a strong dose of humility and self-awareness, "I could never have done this by myself."

But that is how Father Benedict feels. Through Cardinal O'Connor, he helped establish the community, and one of the founding aspects of our development is that the Friars who were called to the priesthood would attend St. Joseph's Seminary in Yonkers, New York.

Q: And that included you?

Father John: Yes, and so I went off into the seminary to start my religious studies. I went in with Bob Scanlon, who just recently passed away, and we were very much together during the first year. But it was the nurse at the seminary that gave me a physical, which we were all required to have, who discovered I was extremely ill with severe advanced hyperthyroid.

Q: That must have been rough to hear.

Father John: Everything then moved in a different direction. I got very involved with doctors and endocrinologists, and before I knew it, my life was spinning out of control. My life was no longer my own. It was in the hands of the doctors, and because my case was very advanced, my condition was life-threatening.

Q: That must have been quite a cross to carry! Plus it had to be hard realizing that your vocation was at risk.

Father John: I had lost a lot of weight, and I was down to about 96 pounds. I was dropping about a pound a week. I was in grave danger. The doctors, with genuine concern and with compassion, told me that I could not live the lifestyle that the Franciscans had adopted. It was too physically challenging for me because I needed special care, a special diet, special balance in my life. The doctors bluntly told me if I stayed there with the Franciscans, I would die. It was that bad.

So I had to go home and recuperate, and when I finally improved, I resumed my priestly studies, but it became very evident I couldn't go back to the CFR community and that strict observance of poverty. So I listened to a lot of good advice, and I went back to St. Joseph's Seminary as a diocesan priesthood candidate.

Q: Which is not a bad choice given the available options...

Father John: Absolutely! But when push came to shove, if that's what the Lord wanted and ultimately I wanted to be a priest, what difference does it make as long as I could become one of His priests? It really did not matter what the avenue or path was, and I loved St. Joseph's Seminary. I had wonderful holy years there that I am truly grateful for.

Q: You have done a lot of the artwork for Father Benedict's books. Tell me how that came about and when did you start painting?

Father John: I have been painting most of my life from childhood. I painted for my needs and for other people. If they wanted a pretty picture done, I would just paint.

But Father Benedict, a well-known author, often expressed his disappointment over the covers that would land on his books. Father Benedict is actually quite artistic, and he has a history of some artistic accomplishment and, in his youth, produced remarkable marquetry of pictures of saints. Several of his works are magnificent and on the walls of Trinity Retreat House in Larchmont, New York. People call them inlays, but they are actually called marquetry, and they are well done.

So from an artistic viewpoint, he discovered by visiting my home that I was artistic because, parents being parents, they hung my work up in lovely frames. When Father Benedict saw them, he was impressed and so he asked me if I would do the cover for his next book.

Q: That must have made you feel great!

Father John: Of course, I was honored, thrilled, and frightened because a book cover is a big deal when you are doing it for a major publishing house. I didn't know if I was up for the task, but I said I would certainly try.

I remember one day at Trinity Retreat, he invited me to come and bring one of my paintings, and I brought one from my parent's house, and I propped it up on a chair. He looked at it for some time in silence, and then he told me, "You're an artist." That was the first time I ever felt like one. Being affirmed and validated, I developed much more confidence to step out and do something for the public.

Q: What was your first artistic cover on a Father Benedict book?

Father John: The first published book I did was for *Stumbling Blocks and Stepping Stones*. I had done that picture for myself because when other college students would go off for Spring Break, which I obviously was not interested in doing some of the activities that they would participate in, I was determined to use that time in order to do something that I could enjoy for the rest of my life.

So what I would do during that short break was delve into a picture, and create my own vision of something from my heart. That was the first picture I did in college, and that was used on the first book.

Q: Do you read Father Benedict's manuscript first and then create the art? Or are you painting at the same time he is writing? How does that process work?

Father John: All I really need to do is just ask him to tell me what he's doing, and he articulates what his intent is and what his vision of the book is. Father Benedict has always been so good at allowing me to form the picture and do what I think. He never imposes any of his own ideas or says something like, "Well, I want you to paint this in a particular fashion."

Q: For an artist, that is always refreshing to hear because in life a lot of projects are dictated and micro-managed down to the minutest detail.

Father John: He knew that would constrict me, so he let me do what I wanted, and that was very freeing. I think an artist does better in that creative environment.

Chapter 4: Fr. John W. Lynch

Q: Have you ever painted something, looked at it and said "No! I can't stand this! Maybe I need to go in a different direction?"

Father John: No, not really.

Q: You have always received positive feedback from Father Benedict?

Father John: I've always gotten good responses. He is like a dream mentor because he always knows what to say and when to say it. You know I was a young person and not filled with a lot of self-confidence, and he made all of the contacts for me to get my work on the cover. It is funny for me to recall entering the Capuchin novitiate because basically, I said, "It's over. My artwork must come to an end because now I'll be a Friar doing many things and will not have any time for art. I must be open to what the Lord's will is and must be willing to follow what other people will tell me what I need to do."

And actually, that sentiment made sense because you don't want to bring your determined visions into religious life. You're there to learn and be led and not bring in your own agenda. So with that mindset firmly in place when I was at the novitiate, that is when I received a phone call from Father Benedict's book publisher asking if they could commission me to do a work about St. John of the Cross. I basically said no because I was letting go of that former part of my life, but I needed to inform the Novice Master that I had received a phone call and was very surprised when he told me, "Go ahead and do it!"

I said okay but inquired to make sure it was not going to be a problem. And he said, "Well, if it becomes a problem, we'll let you know. But if God gave you the gift, use the gift!"

So it is interesting how something like a gift of art can be used by the Lord, because I was determined not to use it as a secular or secondary career. I desired to do something that had spiritual growth and holiness attached to it.

Q: How many book covers have you done?

Father John: Oh, I need to think about that because through Father Benedict, I met others who also wanted me to do artwork for their books. I would say about a dozen. I'm not doing any presently because life as an archdiocesan pastor can be a little busy.

Chapter 4: Fr. John W. Lynch

Q: Do you have a favorite book cover?

Father John: The favorite and nearest and dearest to my heart would be my very first, *Stumbling Blocks and Stepping Stones*, because I designed that out in my head.

Q: Is that normally how you work?

Father John: How I normally work is that I will plan things out of my head, detail by detail, then I will paint it on the canvas. It is interesting to do, and when I am finished with all of the thoughts in my head, it just comes right out onto the canvas.

Q: Do most artists work that way? Have you talked with other artists about their process of painting?

Father John: I really don't know. I know some artists who do extensive study and research. I do that, too, but after the fact. I still just design a picture in my head.

Q: I don't want to lose the chance for you to explain why the cover of *Stumbling Blocks and Stepping Stones* is your favorite. Please share a bit about this.

Father John: There is an interesting story about *Stumbling Blocks and Stepping Stones*, which is clearly a vocational painting. It was meant to be a vocational story because it is about a pilgrim sitting on a cliff, fingering a cross, and he is pondering whether or not to pick up the cross.

In the background are ruins, like you would see in Ireland or England, of something that was once very grand, very glorious. And it's reflected in the water, which in artistic circles often reflects memory, and perhaps there's a certain melancholy.

In the ruins stands a figure, and it is Christ. It is all in silhouette, including the figure of Christ, and He is not reflected in the water. It's a very psychological picture, and I really didn't make up my mind to make it psychological. All I did was just paint my story of what I was feeling at the time in a rather developed fashion. It's not slash-dash. It's very studied and very detailed and carefully worked out, but then again, that is my style.

Q: And what else is in this vocational story?

Chapter 4: Fr. John W. Lynch

Father John: When you look at the picture, you need to ask the question: will this young man, this pilgrim, in his pilgrim robes, pick up that cross?

For me, it meant that I would. I would pick up the cross and follow Christ. And where was Christ in this picture? He was in silhouette studying the ruins. What were the ruins? It sounds sad, so tragic. It's not so tragic, but there was a sadness to it because I knew my vision of the Church and the vision of my vocation was crumbling within me.

Without getting too complex, I could feel my vocation story typifying. It just wasn't what I thought about becoming a priest. It was more and more about Jesus Christ, becoming His servant and the poverty of that. So that painting is all about what was leading my life, all the immature things. My faith was maturing and becoming much more Christ-centered, and the ruins represent childhood and childhood things and how it needs to go.

Q: What kind of feedback did you get from the painting?

Father John: One great story involves Cardinal O'Connor. When the CFRs were developing, he became our spiritual father, with all of the necessary contacts, and he invited us down to the Cardinal's Residence and I went. Father Benedict encouraged me to bring the painting with me.

Q: That was an honor! I hope the painting was okay going through midtown.

Father John: It was finished and framed, suitable for travel, but I asked Father Benedict why he wanted me to bring it along to show the Cardinal. He said to me, "Well, it's on my new book."

It was in 1987, hot off the presses, and he wanted to show off the new artwork, nice and large because you always lose something when the picture is shrunk to fit on the cover, and Father Benedict was very proud of it. So I said, "Okay, I'm willing to bring it, but I hope it's not going to be embarrassing." And Father Benedict said, "No, the Cardinal will be very interested."

Q: It's almost like Father Benedict knew something would happen.

Chapter 4: Fr. John W. Lynch

Father John: Yes! And so I brought the painting, and we were all there at the Cardinal's Residence, beginning a new life as Franciscan Friars of the Renewal, and we were all chattering until the Cardinal made it clear it was time to sit down and talk business.

And just as we all sat down and we were all quiet, he noticed the painting. It was propped up against the chair, and he asked, "What's this?" And Father Benedict explained it was the picture for his newly published book, which, at the time, Brother John had created.

And I really thought the Cardinal would give a very courteous, polite glance and pass it back in order to get on with the business of the day, which was serious business. Instead, he had me pick up the painting and bring it to him across the large beautiful room. I brought it very close to him and propped it on his knees. Instead of saying something, he fell into a long period of silence.

Q: What did you do?

Father John: I began to panic because it was an awkward silence when no one was talking. He was almost getting lost in the painting, and it was obvious to everyone in the room that this was an awkward silence. I panicked because I wasn't ready for the spotlight. Finally, after staring into the picture, he spoke and spoke to the picture. He pointed to it, saying, "This is why I became a priest."

Whatever this vocation picture was for me, it touched him, the Archbishop of New York, and it caused him to get lost in the memory of his own story of becoming a priest and his journey. I'll never forget the trip back, thinking that this humble picture from my humble little world touched the Cardinal! And Father Benedict took note.

Then I remember the Cardinal, efficient as he was, looked at me and said, "Excellent! Whatever you do, don't stop painting! Now let's get on with the business of the day."

Q: Moments like that really affirm an artist, don't they?

Father John: It was extraordinary. How blessed I was to have his attention and to see his personal reaction, which again was made possible through Father Benedict prompting me to bring the painting.

Chapter 4: Fr. John W. Lynch

Q: Let's move ahead and look at you becoming a diocesan priest for the Archdiocese of New York. You are no longer a CFR. How did that change your relationship with Father Benedict?

Father John: I would say it really did not change it at all. In a sense, it gave me greater access to his life because, with the CFR community, we would always have to walk under their umbrella. Since leaving the community Father Benedict and I could go to museums or to the symphony without worrying what the other Friars would say or think about being left out. We have a great friendship because we share a lot of the same interests in fine art and great music and spirituality in the Church. I was smart enough at a young age to let him teach me, and I gleaned as much as I could.

So I would say my diocesan life didn't really change anything. If anything, it just gave our friendship more dimension to share as priests. We also now can speak about priestly concerns because there is a little detachment when one is not a priest. There are certain things that you just can't share.

Q: Your family, particularly your mother and father, seemed also to be drawn very much into Father Benedict as well. Your father has done work with Father Benedict for a number of years. How did that relationship start?

Father John: I had the honor of introducing Father Benedict to my family. It is nice when the teenager brings home someone really wonderful into the family fold, and he has really been a blessing to us.

Until I was ordained, Father Benedict really was our family priest. He was with us through many of the difficult times every family has, including sickness and death. He was there with comforting words and guidance. Whenever my family had a need, he would rush over. Our cup really did runneth over with abundant blessings.

Q: You have had the abundant blessing to do quite a bit of traveling with Father Benedict. If you had to pick one destination as the most inspirational, what would that be?

Father John: Clearly, it would be the Holy Land. At the ripe old age of 18, I started to travel worldwide with Father Benedict. I had an appetite for travel, and

Chapter 4: Fr. John W. Lynch

here he was, giving me a clear-cut role of how I could be helpful, and I was. Through the grace of God and the role that I played, I didn't have to pay for any of it!

I worked my way through his pilgrimages and tours. It wasn't hard work, but it was work, and I was able to go through the Middle East and into Europe, as well as out to California without a dollar in my pocket and met some very important and fascinating people.

Q: Obviously, Father Benedict is known for being an accomplished teacher. Was there anything in particular during your trip with him to the Holy Land that really brought the place alive to you?

Father John: We did make three trips together to the Holy Land, and there are many stories I could tell, but one of the most moving memories is when we went to the house of Caiaphas. Most pilgrims don't go there, but when you do, you see that they have a pit that is dug out of the rock.

It's the basement of the house, which served as a prison, and the archeological studies show that this was Caiaphas' basement. Research indicates that

Christ was kept overnight in this pit which was dark, dank, and inhospitable. In fact, there is an image of Christ in mosaic in the Church of St. Peter in Gallicantu of Christ being lowered by ropes into this very pit.

Now keeping this in mind, Father Benedict, knowing I was his vocation, got special permission and took me down into this blocked-off pit! Down there was an altar. Believe me, it was not festive with marble and statues of angels. This was a hole in the ground. And remember, when Christ was thrown down there, the pit had no staircase. Today there is one there, but not 2,000 years ago.

So Father Benedict arranged for the two of us to go down into a place where we know Christ had been held captive, and he offered Mass with just the two of us right there. I wasn't even a Brother at the time. I was still going to Iona College, but for the first time, I really felt what the priesthood was like in the context of the Mass. Not as one who was attending but as one who was participating. It was a magnificent moment of the priesthood to be, and Father Benedict created that with great deliberate intent.

Chapter 4: Fr. John W. Lynch

Q: The way you describe that I can really see how much of a mentor Father Benedict was in your early years...

Father John: And there were so many other marvelous memories that mark your soul when you visit the Holy Land. Mass is never the same. Scripture is never the same. The visit really does change everything.

Q: Let's change gears and talk about Mother Teresa. There are a million Mother Teresa stories, but I'd like to hear yours and how Father Benedict made that connection.

Father John: It was hilarious because they were very close friends. Through Father Benedict, I was given a great deal of access to Mother Teresa to the point where he would frequently call, whether I was at school or at home, and say, "Come on down right away. Mother Teresa is coming!" (laughter)

I was given great access to her, and after a while, I began to feel very comfortable around her, but every time I was with her, I knew I was with someone truly different. Holy? Yes, but she had a searing focus on Jesus Christ. When you were with her, you felt that He was standing right next to her. She was that familiar with Christ.

Q: So you had a very interesting dynamic being in the same room with Mother Teresa and Father Benedict.

Father John: Well, Father Benedict was familiar with Mother Teresa. I was familiar with Mother Teresa. And she was familiar with Jesus. Of course, she had a great sense of awe and mystery about Christ, but He was just there and you caught that spirituality. Her accessibility to Christ was tremendous.

She always had this large collection of miraculous medals, and she wanted everyone to have them. Over the years, I received many of them from her so that I could in turn give them away, which I did. Mother Teresa would take each medal and kiss each one. She never gave away any of the Miraculous Medals before reverently kissing it.

Her faith was alive. She walked with Jesus. She lived with Him and loved Him and really was in relationship with Him.

Chapter 4: Fr. John W. Lynch

Q: Was it unnerving when you hit the street or went outside of a church and multitudes of people were there to see her? How did you handle the crowds?

Father John: Well, Mother Teresa handled the spotlight better than anyone I ever saw. She was not impressed with adulation, and there was no change in her from when you saw her alone or if she was surrounded by people. I, on the other hand, had a real change of demeanor when I was in crowds and people were pushing and shoving in order to get near her.

I didn't like it. But with her, there was no change in her expression or voice. To her, there was no crowd. She dealt with people one to one and saw Christ in that person who she spoke with. I was with her many times in crowds of people, and the crowds bothered me, but they never bothered her. I was aware of the crowds, but she wasn't. That's the difference between the two of us, and Father Benedict is the same way. When I see a crowd, psychologically, I want to get away from it, but it doesn't bother him.

Father Benedict will strike up a conversation with anyone in a crowd. Any stranger, and before you know it, within five minutes, you will think they are longtime friends because they have shared family history and personal information. They have made some connection, as obscure as it may be, and suddenly they are related. It's amazing.

It is one of his gifts, and I think that's why Father Benedict and Mother Teresa got along so well. Even though they were from two different worlds: Jersey City and Calcutta; they both knew how to relate to people, and they both were devoted to Christ. And I think that's why she trusted Father Benedict so much and confided in him and vice versa. They were like brother and sister and had a marvelous connection and friendship.

Q: Well, we've had a very nice conversation up to this point, but I do want to delve into some painful remembrances because you were with Father Benedict during his January 2004 accident in Orlando, Florida. Can you walk our readers through your recollection of that day?

Father John: We were traveling to Orlando, Florida, because Father Benedict was giving a retreat. I was with him along with David Burns, who works at

Chapter 4: Fr. John W. Lynch

Trinity Retreat, and oddly enough, we were early in our arrival there at the Orlando airport.

The line for our rental car pickup was very long. In fact, it was jammed, and I had never seen so many people waiting for cars. So David got on line for the rental car, and I stayed with the luggage.

Father Benedict saw the long line David was on, and he told me he was going to go make a phone call to a bishop outside where it would be less noisy, so he went. I would have preferred that he stayed inside the terminal where I could keep an eye on him, but I figured he had done this hundreds of times before around the world, so it was no big deal.

So time passed, and after a while, I began to receive a strange feeling, an intuition that something was not right, and I said to myself, "Where's Father Benedict?"

Now he wasn't outside for very long, but I just started to get concerned, and I do have a mother hen connection to him and worry about him, so I waved to David, who was still in the long rental car line and, with hand signals, told him I was going outside to look for Father Benedict. It was risky because I was leaving our luggage unattended, but David motioned to me that it was okay.

Keep in mind that the security at the airport is always announcing not to leave your luggage unattended and for people to report it if they see any unclaimed luggage around. So you can realize how concerned I was to go outside and look for him. So I went outside the terminal and looked around, and he was not there. At that point, I am like, "Forget the luggage!"

I went around the building twice. I went to the dumpsters and looked around. I couldn't figure out where he would be! I went back inside the terminal and began asking strangers if they had seen a man dressed in a gray robe who looked like a monk. I knew if I described him, it would be clear to those who may have just seen a glimpse of him. No one saw him, and it was clear he had not come back in.

So now I was getting upset, and I began pacing. I went over everything in my mind, and I definitely knew he was in trouble, but I wasn't really sure what it was. Father Benedict had wandered off before but never for such a long period of time. So I prayed to the Holy Spirit, "Just tell me where he is! You know I am upset. We don't know anyone down here. Just tell me where he is!"

Chapter 4: Fr. John W. Lynch

And it had to be the Holy Spirit who answered because I heard something say to me, "Go that way." I looked, and that way was a dark highway, which was eight lanes, four one-way and four lanes in the opposite direction, and it was extremely busy with traffic. I thought that he couldn't be there because it was just a highway, but the message I received told me to go that way, and so I did.

I began jogging along, and then I started running alongside this highway, and before I knew it, I jumped over this hedge and was running across four lanes of a busy highway, almost getting hit myself! I got to the median and continued running.

Now I had gotten pretty far from our terminal because I do jog and run, and I can move at a pretty good clip, and so I was running down this dark highway at probably 8:30 at night, and I am thinking, "Have I lost my mind? What am I doing?"

And then I saw something ahead of me down the highway. I saw police lights. Now mind you, I had no reason to think it was Father Benedict because I had gone so far from our terminal, but I knew to run further.

Thinking back on everything now, it is amazing that in the time we were waiting for him, he really did walk that far and was in the process of getting us dinner, which, thank God, we never asked for so that we would not have any guilt. We never said to him, "We're hungry!"

Q: He was just trying to be nice.

Father John: Yes, he later told us he was trying to surprise us by getting dinner. So I knew I needed to go toward the swirling red police car lights, and so I ran like lightning.

When I got there, the police had created this protective circle, and I tried to break through. They stopped me, and so I tried again.

Somehow, I knew Father Benedict was inside that circle, but I also knew that if I tried a third attempt, the police would arrest me. So I said, "Excuse me, I am looking for an older man dressed in a gray robe. He has a gray beard. He has a rope around his waist and is wearing sandals. Have you seen him?"

And immediately, they took me inside their circle. The ambulance had just arrived, and now I was valuable to them. I wasn't just this crazy guy who was trying to cause chaos. I could help them and identify this nameless person who had just been struck by a

Chapter 4: Fr. John W. Lynch

car. Thankfully, I had a clear enough mind, and I knew his life was hanging by a very thin thread.

I knew I needed to earn the trust of the officers, and I asked if I could see him. I explained I was traveling with him and was responsible for him, but then I remembered David, and so I asked one of the officers if they could drive me back to the terminal to get David because I didn't want to leave him there, and I didn't know what shape he would be in when he learned the news of what happened.

Q: And what were the officers saying to you?

Father John: They told me right then that it was a potential fatality. They weren't holding anything back. But, somehow, through the grace of Jesus Christ, I knew I was going to be the tool that was going to be used to help him get through this and survive. He was in a grave condition, but I wasn't accepting that, and that's how I was keeping my cool and getting through the ordeal.

The police officer was wonderful. She drove me back to the terminal where we picked up David and then drove the two of us to the hospital. Father Benedict was in the Trauma Center being worked on, and they would not let anyone in.

Now mind you, I had never been in any situation like this before, but I knew I needed to get in there, and so I went to the desk and insisted on entering, which really is an absurd request, and I was told, "You are not allowed in there. The doctors are working on him."

But something impelled me to get in there, regardless of whatever it took. The woman at the desk kept saying no, and so I said, "Thank you very much," and I went to the police who were there. I knew they needed to help me because of what had transpired, and I had remained calm and professional. I thanked them profusely. We were building up a comfort level where they seemed to be trusting me, and I certainly trusted them. So I went up to them and said, "Listen, there has to be a way for me to get into the Trauma Center to be with Father Benedict. I am his representative. He has a lot of medical issues that I know about, and I can speak for him. I can answer questions that the doctors may have. Please help me get in there so I can help him."

Chapter 4: Fr. John W. Lynch

The police were wonderful. They said, "Okay, we'll try to get you in, but it is their call because it is their territory."

So the police went with me up to the desk, and I again stated that I needed to be in there to help. The police aided me by saying that they would go in with me, and I would be under their supervision, and so they agreed.

We walked down a long sterile hall into the unit, and there was Father Benedict. And it wasn't a pretty sight. It was sheer horror. His bones were broken. There was blood everywhere. It was like a scene from Vietnam. It was that bad.

So when I got into the room, I introduced myself to who I thought was the head nurse, because as soon as the police escorted me to where Father Benedict was, I was left alone. I said, although I had no experience in any of this, I am offering myself in any way to help.

Q: Did you tell them that you were a priest?

Father John: I'm sure I did. The head nurse then said, "Are you willing to do this?" And this was to clear Father Benedict's passageway so he wouldn't choke.

I said yes and asked her to show me how, because I had never done it before. The nurse was very patient with me and showed me exactly how to do it, and I picked it up right away. So I was doing that and dabbing his mouth.

It wasn't pleasant, but I was happy to help, and before you knew it, they were treating me as part of the team. They asked me if I would help with x-rays. Because I was keeping my cool outwardly, they trusted me, and I blended in. I was being useful to them.

They said to me, "We have to dress you up if you're going to help us like this." So they had me put on a heavy gown with special materials so that I wouldn't be hurt by the x-ray machinery as I was holding up the boards for the technicians.

They accepted me as an extra pair of hands, and they worked straight through the night. Talk about a vigil! It was a constant battle to help keep him alive. As soon as they leveled him and secured his vital signs, he would crash. His blood pressure, his respiration, his heart rate – everything would go down and crash. He'd flat line and they would need to go back and try to get him to a stable condition. The

Chapter 4: Fr. John W. Lynch

medical team was extraordinary in how they really fought for his life.

There were interesting scenarios where he would crash, and the doctors and nurses would just sort of dive on this bloody, broken body that was basically the color of ash most of the time. He did look like a corpse, and they would dive on him and work on him very efficiently, but there was a certain look of violence to their actions because they were so quick and dramatic, and there was quite a bit of yelling as they worked.

Q: And how did you handle these episodes?

Father John: For me not to get in the way, I would dive under the gurney. I had the presence of mind to get under the gurney every time it happened. Now that I look back on it, what an absurd posture to be in, but I did not want to be a hindrance and was happy to be there because I knew I was nearby and could be helpful.

So it was a very long night, and Father Benedict crashed one last time, and I knew what the medical team was thinking. They had been so valiant in bringing him back and stabilizing him so many times. I heard that snapping sound of the rubber gloves coming off and of course, you can't touch a patient after you take the gloves off. The doctor said, "That's it. We're done. Let him go."

I lunged at the doctor, not to hurt him, but I said to him, "Go back! Don't stop! Go back!" Suddenly this calm, rather professional stranger who was dressed like an Oxford technician and who had done a good job at blending in was now acting like a protective lion that was trying to save his cub that was broken and bruised. And I kept saying, "Go back!"

I remember him looking at me. This tired doctor, who had worked so hard and who earned a gold medal, as they all did, for their effort. He had a look that said I was asking too much. But I could not, in any way, accept the loss of Father Benedict. Death was not an option.

The doctor looked at me with that tired, frustrated, angry look, and there was a long pause. It was a stare-down. He stared at me, and I stared right back at him and said, "Go back!" And the doctor turned and put his gloves back on. I went into a sublime period of prayer where I knew I was with Christ. He wasn't far away. Christ was right there beside me in

Chapter 4: Fr. John W. Lynch

that Trauma Center. We were together. In that time, I begged Him to please spare Father Benedict's life and to bring him back.

The monitors were telling a bleak story, and the medical team knew they were going back to what looked like a dead corpse. And I knew, in part, they did go back to him just to shut me up. But they were trying and by the grace of Jesus Christ and through their diligence, there was a flicker of hope.

Father Benedict's life was like the coals of a fire that needed help to be reignited. I begged Jesus Christ to just "Keep it going! Keep that flame of life alive!"

They pushed me away as I stood there so they could work on him. To think of that grace-filled moment that I was allowed to be there because if I were not there, they definitely would not have gone back one more time. But they did go back, and Father Benedict stabilized and remained stable. It was still touch and go, but as soon as he remained stable, they rushed him into the Critical Care Unit, and I had about a 10-minute grace period when I could run out to see David Burns, because I was concerned about him. I did manage to get David in to see Father Benedict. He asked me what he should do, and I told him, "Just stand in the corner and pray."

He had already been praying all night, but it was good for him to be there and to add in the intercessory prayer.

When we finally left the Trauma Center, I knew that Christ had brought Father Benedict back from death and that we were on our way. I knew it would be a rocky road, and it did turn out to be far rockier than I ever could imagine, but somehow I knew he had been saved from the clutches of death. Christ had saved him.

The doctors did later come to me and said there was a problem with toxins in his body. Father Benedict's color was turning yellow, and I watched as his body was swelling as it filled up with toxins, to the point that it became grotesque.

So there was an option to do surgery, but it would be exploratory with no guarantees because they weren't sure what was wrong.

So I told them to go ahead and Father Benedict was in surgery for several hours, and I knew things did not go well. The doctors told me that the internal

Chapter 4: Fr. John W. Lynch

injuries had not caused the toxic infection, but they still weren't sure what the cause was and that there was nothing else that could be done. Then I was told to make final preparations.

So I knew what I needed to do again. I needed to be his advocate, and so I turned to Christ and said, "You are going to have to do it again."

The nurses stopped coming in, and his room in CCU was like a glass cage, so I assigned an angel to each corner of his room to pray for Father Benedict's recovery.

Now I'm not what you would call a charismatic priest, but I really felt inspired to pray over Father Benedict. I fell into a state of prayer, and I called on the Holy Name of Jesus and the power of the Holy Spirit for the toxins to leave his body.

I prayed over him without touching him, because if I did touch him, his skin was so tight it would have burst. But my prayer and the words were going over his body and massaging him.

Some of the nurses who walked by saw me and stopped to watch me pray. They were curious and wondered what I was doing, but they were respectful. And in the middle of the night, one of the nurses came to me and said Father Benedict's condition was improving, but they didn't know why. Then she looked at me and said, "Whatever you are doing, don't stop!"

Now they were not Catholic. Some of the medical staff may not have even been Christian, but they were all good people, and they knew that this prayer and the invocation of the Name of Jesus Christ were working. And I wasn't doing it in a flamboyant manner. I was calm, and I was just praying in a very confident way. By the next morning, the toxins in Father Benedict's body were gone.

Q: Awesome! Were you praying to any saints as well?

Father John: No, the funny thing was later I actually had a prayerful apology session to some of my favorite saints because I hadn't called upon them. I felt that I really needed to just focus on the Name of Jesus and I was really focused on Him as the Divine Physician. My prayer was very personal. I wanted Father Benedict back, not for the world. I wanted him back for me. And I received a wonderful affirmation that Jesus does want us to have a close personal devotion to Him alone and develop a confident faith.

The irony was that as Jesus healed Father Benedict, I was being transformed and touched. Going through that tunnel of fire with Christ changed me forever, and I will never be the same again.

Q: Did you notice any changes in the nurses or doctors after Father Benedict was healed?

Father John: Absolutely! Now they were always very professional and good, but as they saw my prayer with Father Benedict and then eventually with the Friars who came down from New York and with Marjule, Father Benedict's sister, the staff was very impressed.

Some of them were quite surprised and were asking things like, "What is that thing you are doing?" And we would tell them it is prayer and they would be astonished.

One doctor came up to me and said, "Father John, we are a team, right?" And I said yes, and he continued, "As a member of the same team you need to keep doing what you are doing, and we will keep doing what we are doing, and Father Benedict will be just fine!"

And they did give credit to God. It was such a witness for them to see Jesus heal Father Benedict. It was also good for the other patients in the hospital who heard what was going on, too.

Q: And all of this leads to the fact that we are celebrating Father Benedict's 50th anniversary. With all that you have been through with your very close friend, what kind of thoughts can you share about this great milestone?

Father John: I'm just so blessed by the walk I have had and, thank God, still have. I thank God because it has been the ultimate education. I have learned so much from him.

He has really re-defined priesthood for me. He is so devoted to Christ. He is Christ's best friend. The love he has for Christ affected me and has helped me in my relationship. His devotion to the Eucharist is awe-inspiring.

You know Father Benedict is a priest from head to toe. If you were to run DNA on him, you'd find that he is completely a priest, and he is completely connected to Christ in every way.

Chapter 4: Fr. John W. Lynch

We all have places inside us that we reserve just for ourselves. You can call them little rooms inside of you. Even we priests have them.

But Father Benedict?

He doesn't have that. I know it for a fact. He really is devoted and consumed by Christ. That's how and why he can do all that he does. We all joke about where he gets the strength and energy to keep the schedule he does. He's like the Energizer Monk, which is a takeoff of the Energizer Bunny that keeps going and going and going...

But Father Benedict does everything he does for Christ. Long ago he beat away his ego, and he has given Christ permission to work through him.

Chapter 5

Fr. Andrew Apostoli, CFR

Father Andrew Apostoli, CFR, was one of eight founding members of the Franciscan Friars of the Renewal. He taught for 28 years at St. Joseph's Seminary in Dunwoodie, New York, and served as Vice-Postural for the Cause of Venerable Fulton J. Sheen, as well as acting as Spiritual Advisor for various ministries including the World Fatima Apostolate. Father Andrew authored several books and hosted the EWTN series "Sunday Night Prime."

Q: Do you remember the first time you met Father Benedict?

Father Andrew: I'm not sure if it was at one of his classes. He was giving classes for priest confessors. He was teaching a class at Dunwoodie for priests who wanted to have some ideas on spirituality for confessors. It was an excellent course, and I think that may have been the first time I saw him.

You see, he belonged to the New York/New England Province of the Capuchins. I belonged to the New Jersey Province, and there wasn't a whole lot of contact between our two provinces.

But I did hear about him for many years. In fact, when I was a student, they talked about this Friar, and the irony of it was the first six years after my ordination I spent in New Jersey, and then I went up to Beacon, New York, and I started meeting people who told me, "You look like Father Benedict. You sound like Father Benedict, and you even say a lot of things that are similar to him!"

Q: So without even meeting, the Lord was putting the two of you on a similar path.

Chapter 5: Fr. Andrew Apostoli, CFR

Father Andrew: Yes, I guess so, but on a more personal level, it took years when I actually met him at the priests' confessor class, and then he did a retreat for my New Jersey Province.

Q: And that went well?

Father Andrew: It went so well that I felt inspired to want to do work with priests. When I was ordained, Bishop Fulton Sheen said, "If there is any key to the renovation of the Church and the salvation of the world today, it lies in the renewal of the priesthood." I knew Father Benedict did a lot of priest retreats, so I asked him if I could do one. Well, Father Benedict had bypass heart surgery in 1984, and wouldn't you know it, he called me up and asked me to take over the retreat for him! I was just hoping to assist.

Q: Was it a large gathering?

Father Andrew: The retreat had 104 priests and two bishops! (laughter) So that was my first experience, and Father Benedict said to me, "Well, if you're going to make a faux pas, make it a major faux pas!" And that was the start of me really getting to know him.

Q: So the retreat went well?

Father Andrew: Well, Father Benedict said he received good reports from my work on that retreat, and he told me that he knew I could do this work. Not every priest is cut out to minister to other priests, and that's when he asked me if I would come and work with him.

Q: So he needed an assistant?

Father Andrew: Well, the priest that had been assigned with him left to become a pastor at a parish, so yes, he was in need of an assistant, and so he asked if I would work with him.

Q: Now, when were you ordained?

Father Andrew: I was ordained on March 16, 1967.

Q: How long before Father Benedict was that?

Father Andrew: Well, he's 50 years this year, and I'm 42 years, so it is a difference of eight years.

Chapter 5: Fr. Andrew Apostoli, CFR

Q: You have a rich history with Father Benedict. Can you briefly describe a bit of the transition that occurred in leaving the Capuchins and creating this new community that became the Franciscan Friars of the Renewal?

Father Andrew: Well, my part in the discernment as such was pretty minimal. We knew there were a lot of problems, and there were a lot of challenges in the Capuchin Provinces because of the way things were going, and we weren't happy.

Q: How so?

Father Andrew: We realized that there seemed to be more of a secular movement going on and less of an authentic Franciscan spirituality. I was working with Father Benedict, and I'll never forget he came to me one day and said there were some young Brothers that were interested and talking about a renewal, and he asked me if I was interested.

Q: How long did it take you to get on board?

Father Andrew: I knew immediately because I had thought about it years before, but I never did anything. Obviously, I realize now that it takes somebody of the caliber of Father Benedict to do it. First of all, he knew what to do. He had clear insights, and he was a real leader.

He also had contacts, notably Cardinal O'Connor, and so if you are going to get something started, it's good to know some top people that can cut through some of the red tape that occurs as you move up the ladder.

Q: When you made the transition and began this new community of Friars in 1987, there were some who were not exactly happy. There were naturally some Capuchins who were offended. How did that affect you, and how do you think that affected Father Benedict?

Father Andrew: Well, Father Benedict had a lot of friends in the Order, and I think it was a lot harder for him in the sense that he was so close to so many. I think his leaving was more upsetting than my leaving because I did not know as many Capuchins as he did. I mean, I did have friends in the community, but

Chapter 5: Fr. Andrew Apostoli, CFR

the relationships weren't as strong as his were. So, in that sense, I did not suffer as much as he did because he had long-standing friends.

Q: Did you ask any Capuchins to come with you?

Father Andrew: I did ask one Brother to come, and I wanted to ask a second, but for personal reasons, it did not work out.

Q: Let's get back to you so it doesn't get lost that you have 42 years of priestly service. Are you looking forward in eight years to be celebrating your own Golden Anniversary?

Father Andrew: Sure, I hope I make it!

Q: How do you see the priesthood? Many diocesan priests are getting older, and there are fewer and fewer young ones to take their place, but the Franciscan Friars of the Renewal seem to have a good number of young men. How do you explain that?

Father Andrew: Well, I think young people tend to be very idealistic. If they're not idealistic, they're going to be hedonistic. They will be into seeking pleasure in a very selfish way. But there is a very generous streak in young people. The thing is that you need to tap into it. I think that's why Pope John Paul II was so successful in working with youth because he knew how to reach them and challenge them to be very generous.

So I think the young people who come to the Franciscan Friars of the Renewal are looking for a challenge, and they want something authentic. They're looking for something that is very faithful to the Church, and that's something we try to maintain. We also have a very clear identity.

Q: How would you say the identity is perceived?

Father Andrew: A lot of people have told me that when they look at our Friars, they have a clear notion of a very masculine identity. That is being masculine without being macho. They exude a real manly sense about them, and it is a wonderful, self-evident quality. I think young men look for that, and it does attract them.

Chapter 5: Fr. Andrew Apostoli, CFR

Q: Do you see a resurgence in the Church with the men who are being ordained?

Father Andrew: Definitely. I think those who are entering religious life now are much more aware of what they are giving up. I think compared to 50 years ago, when Father Benedict was ordained or when I came along and entered religious life, I didn't know what I was giving up. I hardly had tasted the world, but in my heart I gave it up, and that's why I am still here.

I think that young people today are different because many come into religious life after they've had a major conversion experience, which was uncommon back in my day.

Q: So it is a different sort of man entering the priesthood today?

Father Andrew: Yes, I think so, but they are very generous souls.

Q: When you think about Father Benedict and his priestly life that spans over 50 years, what do you think his legacy will be?

Father Andrew: First of all, of course, the new community of Friars. He was the spearhead of that. I think our community is going to be around for a long time. It seems to me that it does have deep roots, and you know, the deeper the roots our community has, the more it will withstand the problems that almost inevitably come to any new group.

Secondly, Father Benedict will be well thought of for his teaching and the content of his books. The way he blended psychology with spirituality was brilliant. You know I have a brother who told me once, "That's the genius of Father Benedict!" He's able to take the best in traditional spiritual teaching (called the three ways: Purgative, Illuminative, and Unitive) and blend that with the findings of psychology, where it could be blended.

His ideas of active prayer, mystical prayer, and psychology that are in his writings and in his books will mean a great deal to us in the Church for many years.

Q: Talk about Father Benedict's work at Trinity Retreat in Larchmont, New York. I have heard from others that there are a number of men who were on the periphery of leaving the priesthood,

and Father Benedict was able to help them return to active ministry in a productive way. Can you share in a general way the work that was done at Trinity?

Father Andrew: Yes, it was a remarkable sight to see him help brother priests. Remember, he was sent to Trinity Retreat by Cardinal Cooke (former Archbishop of New York) to set up something for priests, and eventually, not only was he feeding them, spiritually speaking, but he also began to do the work at Trinity as a psychologist. He was called upon to review the priests who announced they wanted to leave.

The Holy See requires that in the process of a priest leaving to get a dispensation in order to get married and so on, he would have to speak to a Catholic psychologist, and of course, Father Benedict was in high demand. He spoke with many priests, and some did actually return. So I think Father Benedict will long be remembered for being very dedicated to the priesthood, which is a wonderful quality about him. I think you can say that although he was often in a position to be with those who had broken down in their priestly vocation, Father Benedict served as an instrument of healing.

In fact, I remember this one priest who was waiting to get back into active ministry. This priest's mother had been sick. He needed to take care of her, and then she later died. This priest shared with me one day how much Father Benedict meant to him because of the time he spent, the care, and the strong counsel he provided.

Chapter 6
Fr. Benedict Groeschel, CFR

Father Benedict Joseph Groeschel, CFR, born July 23, 1933, was an internationally known priest, author, psychologist, and weekly television talk show host on the Eternal Word Television Network (EWTN). He also co-founded and served as Chairman of Good Counsel, Inc.'s Board of Directors.

Born Robert Peter Groeschel in Jersey City, New Jersey, he entered the Capuchin order in 1951 and was given the name Benedict Joseph Labre, who was a French Saint during the 18th century. Father Benedict was ordained a priest in 1959 and earned a master's degree in counseling from Iona College in 1964 and a doctorate degree in psychology from Columbia University in 1971.

In 1960, his Capuchin community appointed Father Benedict as Chaplin of Children's Village in Dobbs Ferry, New York, which at the time was the largest residential program for troubled youth in the United States. In 1974, at the request of Terrence Cardinal Cooke, Archbishop of New York, Father Benedict opened Trinity Retreat in Larchmont, New York, providing spiritual direction and retreats for clergy. He subsequently established the Archdiocese of New York's Center for Spiritual Development in 1983, which provides programs and courses for those desiring spiritual growth. In 1987, Father Benedict and seven other Capuchins left their order to begin a new community called the Franciscan Friars of the Renewal, which continues to grow and flourish, including new missionary efforts expanding into Honduras, Mexico, Ireland, and Sudan.

Chapter 6: Fr. Benedict Groeschel, CFR

On January 11, 2004, Father Benedict was struck by an automobile while crossing a street in Orlando, Florida. He received a head injury and broken bones and had no blood pressure, heartbeat, or pulse for about 27 minutes. A few days later, the trauma triggered a near-fatal heart attack. While he was recovering from his injuries, he collaborated with John Bishop on the book There Are No Accidents: In All Things Trust in God. *Although the accident left him with limited use of his right arm and difficulty in walking, he was back out preaching and giving retreats by the end of 2004, and he has continued to keep a full schedule.*

As he told the New York Times nearly four years after his accident: "They said I would never live. I lived. They said I would never think. I think. They said I would never walk. I walked. They said I would never dance, but I never danced anyway."

Q: During this year, when you celebrate your 50th anniversary of ordination to the priesthood, you must be struck with how many things have

changed. You have seen changes in the Liturgy, including the use of the vernacular, and the local Church has been through a lot in these last 50 years. What can you share about your early priesthood memories?

Father Benedict: When I was ordained in 1959, the Catholic Church in the United States was in the midst of a small age of faith. Because of World War I, the Depression, and World War II, many people thought about the vanity of earthly accomplishment, and they thought of eternal things. So people 50 years ago were much more religious in general. Not just Catholics but everybody.

In 1959, Will Herberg, the sociologist, said that 83 percent of all Catholics, 67 percent of all Protestants, and 53 percent of all Jews attended services every week. It was an age of faith, and there were many vocations. Religious orders were growing, and I was ordained in a year when many fellows were going into the seminary and being ordained. It was a marvelous time, and this age lasted until 1968.

Q: What happened in 1968?

Chapter 6: Fr. Benedict Groeschel, CFR

Father Benedict: 1968 was the year of a cultural revolution, not just in China, but across the world. It affected us culturally, educationally, value-wise and religious-wise. We have yet to recover from 1968. It is the John Paul II generation of young people that is seeing a beginning of a recovery from that time.

I am not saying everyone was irreligious; however, people were a lot less religious and religious communities just about disappeared, which was a terrible loss to the Church.

I went to school with religious Sisters for 12 years. They were excellent religious Sisters and very positive role models. They were also very good teachers. I am glad to see that we are now beginning a restoration of religious life. There is a new organization of Sisters – The Council of Major Superiors of Religious Women – and they have about 10,000 members, all of whom wear the habit! And most of whom are very young.

Q: What was the size of your ordained class, and compare that to the size of a typical seminary class today?

Father Benedict: Well, I was ordained with Capuchins, and there were seven of us at ordination. I have no idea how many the Capuchins have ordained this year, but it would never be that large. Some years our new community, the Franciscan Friars of the Renewal, which I belong to, ordain seven or eight, and we're only 20 years old, but we have about 130-140 members right now, and the average age is about 31, and if I drop dead the average age will go down to 29!

Q: When did you know that you wanted to become a priest?

Father Benedict: Well, I knew I was going to be a priest when I was seven years old.

Q: That is pretty young to want to be a priest.

Father Benedict: I didn't want to be a priest. I really wanted to be a fireman, but I had a wonderful Sister of Charity who taught me, Sister Theresa Maria, and every day after school in Jersey City, she went out with a tray or a box filled with hot food.

One day I asked the neighborhood barber, who was on the ground floor of this tenement building,

Chapter 6: Fr. Benedict Groeschel, CFR

why Sister Theresa Maria came with the food, and he said she was there to take care of an old lady who lived up on the top floor. So I decided to check things out.

Now the only movie I had ever seen as a young boy was Snow White & the Seven Dwarfs, which you may recall has in it a very wicked witch. So I got up to the top floor from the fire escape, and I stood on a milk box, and I looked into this tenement apartment. Right in front of me, six inches away, was the wicked witch!

Q: What did you do?

Father Benedict: I jumped off the milk box, ran down the fire escape, and went into Our Lady of Victory Church and to the Altar of Our Blessed Mother. I can still see myself kneeling there with the blue candle, and I said to myself, "Why doesn't that witch kill Sister Theresa Maria?" I wondered about that, and I figured because she is nice to her, and maybe if people were nicer to witches, they wouldn't be so bad. So something inside of me then said, "Be a priest."

Q: And so you forgot about being a fireman?

Father Benedict: No, I still wanted to be a fireman because near us in Jersey City was the firehouse, and the fire engines were really beautiful. The firemen were always nice to us kids, and they would give us candy. We used to wait around for an alarm just to see them shimmy down the pole. But something inside of me wanted to be a priest, and I listened.

Q: What did your parents say when you told them at seven that you felt a calling to the priesthood?

Father Benedict: I didn't say anything, but in the third grade another Sister gave me a holy picture, and she wrote on the back, "Ora Pro Me," which means Pray For Me. My dad saw the picture, and he asked why did the Sister write that in Latin? I told him that I didn't know and so he told me to go ask her.

So I went and asked, and she said, "Because you are going to be a priest." And since then, I never thought about being anything else but a priest.

Q: Well, you did think about being a psychologist. How did that come about?

Chapter 6: Fr. Benedict Groeschel, CFR

Father Benedict: No, I never thought about being a psychologist. That developed because when I became ordained, I was working with an agency for disturbed children, a therapeutic agency, and it seemed helpful to get a degree in counseling, and the Brothers who taught me encouraged me to get a doctorate so that I could teach in the seminary.

Q: And you went to Columbia?

Father Benedict: Yes, I went to Columbia University, and I was treated very well, very respectfully, and I only have the most positive memories during my time there.

Q: And how has being a psychologist affected your priesthood?

Father Benedict: It has kept me terribly busy! To be a priest and a psychologist at the same time means that the world will beat an eight-lane highway to your door! So I have been incredibly busy doing personality assessments to see if people should become religious. I do a lot of counseling and psychotherapy, and I teach. During these many years, 45 years, I'm teaching pastoral counseling in the seminary. So I guess you can say I got a lot out of my degrees.

Q: Indeed! When you think about the current crisis with the shortages of priests, what can we do about it, or what would you recommend be done?

Father Benedict: Well, you have to look at places where there isn't a crisis. The Diocese of Paterson, New Jersey, has 55 seminarians. It's a little diocese, but the Bishop works very hard on getting vocations. He's very personable. Other dioceses like St. Louis and St. Paul in Minnesota also have large seminaries. I think the seminarians will come if they feel that there is a personal interest in them.

In other dioceses, it can be very difficult. New York is a very tough place for anyone to get vocations. Our community has 17 Novices that have joined this year. Only one Novice is from New York, and only three are from the greater metropolitan New York area. So it is a tough place because New York is a worldly place, but I think it is getting better.

Q: Are all 17 Novices going to study for the priesthood?

Father Benedict: Some of our Novices will be Brothers, but most of them will become priests. I do think that the Church has to rely on Permanent Deacons. Thank God we have them, and also lay people have taken much more of a leadership role in parish life which is very good. A rectory now is a very busy place with people coming and going. Sometimes they need to move the parish offices out of the rectory just to have a little peace. In the old days, the rectory was a place where you went to get a Mass card from a grouchy old Irish housekeeper. Now it's a whole new world!

Q: Let's go back to when you decided to become a priest. What kind of reaction or what kind of support did you get from your parents?

Father Benedict: Oh, my parents were devoted people. They were totally supportive. They didn't know why I wanted to be a Capuchin, which is an order that takes care of the poor, at least it did in those days. My father really wanted me to become a Jesuit.

Q: And why was that?

Father Benedict: He wanted me to join because he had gone to a Jesuit school, as did all of my uncles. But I wanted to work with the poor, and I have been able to do that part-time over the years and especially with Good Counsel and some other programs.

Q: What was your mother's reaction when you told her you wanted to become a priest?

Father Benedict: Oh, she knew all along! She knew with me right when I was seven! In those days, if your mother had a choice between you being President of the United States or you becoming a Catholic priest, it took about a third of a second for her to make up her mind.

Q: Really?

Father Benedict: Parents were greatly honored to have a priest come out of their family. And you know even Protestant and Jewish friends rejoiced with you when you became a priest. I had so many Jewish friends that I gave a blessing at my first Mass in Hebrew! They showed up in droves!

Q: Were there any other relatives of yours that entered religious life?

Father Benedict: I did have a cousin who became a priest, and he is now deceased.

Q: You have written many books. I can't even count how many there are, especially if you were to count the ones that you have written the Introductions for! Is there one particular book that stands out and you can say, "Yes! This is where I really made a contribution!"

Father Benedict: I only write books to do spiritual direction for people in order to help them in their spiritual life, and I just published my 34th book which is to help people who have a tragedy or a disaster in their life. The book is called *The Tears of God*.

The most popular book I wrote is *Arise from Darkness*. It's about difficulty and faith. Not everyone has catastrophes, but everyone has difficulties and sorrow.

So I write to help people, and I never read my books ever. I never watch myself on television. It's appalling! So when you launch a book, it's like having a baby. It goes out and starts its own independent life.

Q: A number of years ago, you wrote a fascinating book about Marian Apparitions. You stated the vast majority of people who report apparitions never get proven, and probably most of the people may be a bit overly emotionally charged and perhaps not really experiencing a true heavenly encounter. Can you expand on that?

Father Benedict: When it comes to reported private revelations, which may not be apparitions, it usually is an inner voice that people hear, or they start writing and don't know what they are writing, but it comes out very well.

Once in a rare while, you will get someone who sees something. I wrote the book *A Still, Small Voice: A Practical Guide on Reported Revelations*, which you refer to. Really, the great authority on this is a Jesuit priest, Father Augustine Poulain, who wrote a hundred years ago, that for every ten revelations reported, one is studied, and for every ten that is studied, one is taken seriously.

It is interesting to note that the Catholic Church universally in 300 years has not approved the private revelation if the person who received it was an adult and their identity was known at the time of their death. People like St. Faustina, St. Margaret Mary, and St. Catherine Laboure, all who were not known. Children are known, like the children of Fatima or Bernadette, because in their naiveté, they told what happened.

Q: In your 50 years of priesthood, you must have had one or two people tell you that they have had a private revelation or other similar experience. How do you handle it?

Father Benedict: I always listen respectfully when a person tells me their account, and I do receive a great many in the mail, and I do look them over. I couldn't study them because I don't have the time. To study one accurately, if you are a psychologist with religious training, would take about ten years.

So in my book, I suggest to people they consider these things religious experiences and that they keep them to themselves, but many people aren't wise enough to take this advice. People who go around loudly proclaiming their private revelations only cause me to have one reaction: I flee!

Q: Now, about 25 years ago, one man by the name of Christopher Bell felt a revelation or an inner desire to help homeless, pregnant women, and he asked you to help with the formation of Good Counsel Homes. How did you come to meet Chris Bell?

Father Benedict: Now, what Chris experienced was not a revelation. It was a profound religious experience, properly called an inspiration. That's very different, having a call to do something. So Chris felt this very strong inclination and need to do it, and he obviously dedicated his life to it very consistently in difficult times, in the face of much opposition, and I was very pleased and honored to be with him almost all of the steps of the way.

Good Counsel is Chris's full-time responsibility; it's not mine. I have many others, but I think an immense amount of untold good has come about because of Good Counsel. We really don't know the number of people, girls, and women, whose lives have been positively affected, and through them, many other people. You know, when you change a person's life for the better, it affects their children, grandchildren, and great-grandchildren. The efforts of what you've done may last for a century.

Having worked with poor people all of my life, I know to reverse the cycle of poverty is never easy. Getting someone on their feet with self-respect and responsibility is very difficult to do, but when it does happen, it changes things dramatically.

Q: You worked at Children's Village in Dobbs Ferry for a number of years. Do you see a correlation between Good Counsel's mission and the work you were doing at Children's Village?

Father Benedict: I worked for 14 years as a chaplain at Children's Village. It's very different from Good Counsel. There were boys, mostly teenagers, all the way up to 17 or 18. And you know, some of them I am still in touch with! In fact, one of them is currently working on the front yard here at Trinity Retreat House as we speak, and he's a man almost 50 years old. He's a grandfather now, but he was my altar boy back when I was at Children's Village. I do see men now who were boys with me at Children's Village, and that brings home to me the good that can be done by an intelligent agency that has the money to do what it needs to do.

You can't do this without money. You need to have staff members, and you need to have staff members around the clock, 168 hours a week.

So I think Good Counsel has done an admirable job. Obviously, if we had all volunteers as years ago when we had all Sisters, we would do a different type of job, but the people who come need to make a living. They have their own family and a home, and so it is a somewhat different perspective as it was at Children's Village.

It is a hard job working with the mothers and children we have at Good Counsel and the youngsters that were at Children's Village. It does take patience, courage, determination, and heart.

Q: When you think about Good Counsel in 2010 celebrating 25 years and all of the work it has done, particularly the pro-life outreach, was this something that resonated inside your heart?

Chapter 6: Fr. Benedict Groeschel, CFR

Father Benedict: Well, I have always been a protestor against infanticide, against abortion, and many times on Saturday mornings, I have been out on the line peacefully and prayerfully protesting. Since we started our new community, many of the Brothers and Sisters are out on Saturday mornings and at other times at local abortion clinics.

Q: Are you still able to go?

Father Benedict: Well, as many people know, since I had a serious accident, I can't do it anymore. I don't have the leg power. So many times when I would be out on Saturday mornings, I heard those in favor of abortion saying, "Well, what are you going to do for the women? Are you going to take care of this kid?"

And the answer is we are prepared. And I could accept a criticism of irresponsibility if a person isn't doing anything. It's one thing to keep a person alive; it's another thing to help them live. I think the proper care of a homeless mom is absolutely essential and the work of God.

When it is not done, we have what Jesus says in the Gospel of St Matthew: I was hungry and you did not give me something to eat. I was a stranger and you did not take me in. I was sick and in prison and you did not visit me. So it is a very serious social responsibility.

Q: Please put on your psychologist hat for a moment and reflect on someone who performs abortions or even promotes abortions to pregnant women. Do you see anything in this group of people psychologically that enables them to do what they are doing?

Father Benedict: Well, I don't know anyone who is performing abortions.

Q: Well, how about someone like Dr. Bernard Nathanson? Many will remember him as an early abortion provider who then had a dramatic conversion experience.

Father Benedict: Well, someone like Dr. Nathanson, by the grace of God, came to a realization that what they were doing was wrong. He certainly penitentially confessed the terrible crime he was involved in and was publicly involved in making amends. But it's not just the abortionists. It's also the politicians, the lawmakers, and the media.

How does this happen? This is a country of fairly altruistic people. This is not Nazi Germany. This is a country of people who care, at least think they care, about their neighbor.

How does this happen? It is simple. People are deceived. The American people, who set up a democracy, home of the free and the brave, tolerated the worst form of corporal slavery in the history of the world. The slavery of black people in the United States is without parallel any place after the Roman Empire. And nice people did it!

Slaves were treated as property, and in 1858, the Supreme Court said that Dred Scott was a chattel, a piece of furniture, and of course, that precipitated the U.S. Civil War.

Q: It is interesting that many current historians do not make a link between the Dred Scott Decision and the decision of Roe v. Wade...

Father Benedict: The U.S. Supreme Court gave us the Civil War and when you look at Roe v. Wade, it has caused incredible disruption politically, socially, and economically in the United States, so candidates win or lose depending on their attitude and position on abortion.

I'm sure the Supreme Court in 1973 thought they were going to solve the whole thing, but they actually opened a terrible wound and many people are deceived.

Q: Can you elaborate a bit more on this deception?

Father Benedict: Well, you need to ask the question of who is doing the deceiving. Who deceived the American people about slavery? Who deceives them now about abortion? Who did Christ say?

The prince of liars: Satan. He is diabolical, seductive, and the master of deception. And this is why nice people do it because even nice people can be deceived. I think every nation, at one time or another, has been deceived. Great Britain would tell you that India is British. India is British?! That's a complete deception.

There were people who defended slavery because it took good care of the slaves. I recently read a quotation from an old book where the author was defending slavery because the slaves couldn't take care

Chapter 6: Fr. Benedict Groeschel, CFR

of themselves! It's a gigantic deception! And now we have abortion.

Q: So what do you think the outcome will be?

Father Benedict: Well, the Supreme Court brought us the Civil War so they may also bring us other catastrophes, and with the complete failure to legislate public morality to protect the young from the vicious media, a complete failure to respect the family and to defend the family, we will be facing many deceptions for quite some time.

Now we are also talking about same-sex marriage, which of course, is a contradiction of terms. What will we do? The old Romans had a saying, "The mills of God grind slowly, but they grind exceedingly fine."

We may be preparing ourselves for a terrible catastrophe of huge proportions and the end of the American experiment. Long ago Benjamin Franklin, who himself was not a devout man, said this government would only work with religious people.

I see European governments sliding into oblivion right now. What will become of Germany? Will they survive? It is estimated that by 2020 Berlin will be a

Muslim City. I'm not unhappy because at least the Muslims pray!

We may be digging our own graves, but if we do survive, we certainly will not survive as an Anglo nation because the Anglos are not contributing to the population, and many are being slaughtered by abortion.

Q: Let's change gears and talk about something or actually someone else. You had a wonderful relationship with Mother Teresa of Calcutta. Many people know that Mother Teresa was one of the great outspoken voices of life. In February of 1994, at the National Prayer Breakfast in Washington, DC, with President and Mrs. Clinton attending, she told them, "Any country that accepts abortion is not teaching its people to love. This is why the greatest destroyer of love and peace is abortion." She then concluded her remarks by stating, "If you become a burning light of justice and peace, you will be true to what the founders of this country stood for." Can you share how you first met Mother Teresa and how your relationship blossomed?

Chapter 6: Fr. Benedict Groeschel, CFR

Father Benedict: Well, I was assigned by Cardinal Cooke to be a liaison between Mother Teresa, her Sisters of Charity, and the Archdiocese of New York. I did get to know her very well, but you know she was not well known back in 1965 when I first met her.

Mother Teresa was a most unusual person, and I knew she was always very serious. It was only after her death, with the publication of her letters to her spiritual director, that we learned how much dark personal sufferings she had endured.

I had heard Mother say many times, and it is true, no nation can survive that kills its own children. Can you imagine any statement more obviously true?

Mother Teresa had no great investment in what we call Western Civilization. In fact, in many ways she was an Indian. You know, when someone asked Mahatma Gandhi what he thought of Western Civilization, he said, "It's a wonderful idea! Why don't they try it?" We always need to remember that God is neither an Anglo, nor an Indian, nor a Black. He is beyond all these things. But He is good, and He is holy, and He is just.

Q: Thank you, Father Benedict, for reflecting on so many things, including your 50th anniversary and about Good Counsel Homes.

Father Benedict: You're welcome, and I want to say that I have a great saying for those who are thinking about helping Good Counsel Homes. It is from St. Vincent de Paul: "Love the poor, and your life will be filled with sunlight, and you will not be frightened at the hour of death."

A few years ago, I was at the hour of death. I was medically dead for 27 minutes. I was unconscious for three weeks, and when I go back over that experience, I know it is true because I was not frightened at the hour of death.

Epilogue

Fr. Fidelis Moscinski, CFR

Fr. Fidelis Moscinski, CFR, is a successor to Fr. Benedict Groeschel, CFR, as Chairman of Good Counsel homes. Fr. Fidelis also leads pro-life ministry for the Franciscan Friars of the Renewal. He is actively involved in Red Rose Rescue to save unborn children.

I was a newly professed brother and only with the Franciscan Friars of the Renewal maybe a year at most. I knew I had to be on my best behavior. I was just trying to get through the next hurdle.

Here was the founder of the community in the car. I was driving; he was sleeping. I looked in the rearview mirror and saw red and white flashing lights. It was one of our New Jersey State Troopers, who are, generally speaking, very serious law enforcement officers. My heart began to pound.

I wasn't aware that I had done anything wrong. But now I had to pull over and wake up Father Benedict – and I was dreading that. "Father Benedict, I'm so sorry, but we just got pulled over by a State Trooper…"

You know how it is when you first wake up unexpectedly. Maybe you don't know exactly where you are. But Father Benedict had a solution. He said, "Well, if you step out of the car, he'll see your habit – then he'll go easier on us."

I said, "Father Benedict, you're not supposed to do that – that's not a good idea." That's when he got his "Father Benedict Face" and said…

"Step. Out. Of the car."

Now I was stuck between a rock and a hard place: the founder who had the power of life and death over me religiously speaking, and a man with a gun right behind me. There was no argument – I opened the door.

I was still sitting in the driver's seat and put one foot on the pavement when over the loudspeaker came, "GET BACK IN THE CAR."

I closed the car door.

I just looked at Father Benedict. I didn't say anything.

He didn't say anything…

One day I was applying to enter the seminary. As a seminarian, you're supposed to get letters of recommendation. I figured, what better person could I get to recommend me than Father Benedict? He was one of the faculty members at the seminary, and everybody knew him; he was famous.

He wrote this letter to the rector:

Dear Monsignor Sullivan,

This letter is a formal recommendation of Brother Fidelis Moscinski, CFR, who is applying as a student for our community through the Archdiocese of New York. Brother Fidelis, as you can tell from his academic record, is an outstanding student and a very fine religious...

He said some other complementary things.

As a courtesy, he gave me a copy of the letter with a note that included, "This letter is all lies!" Father Benedict never lost his sense of humor – he always was able to make us laugh.

At the end of his life, I was taking care of him quite a bit after his accident. He had a very difficult time with mobility. I was traveling with him on this very tiny plane. The aisle was very narrow.

At that time when you were traveling with Father Benedict, he had different cushions due to his broken bones and other problems. He also had a wheelchair and his bag, and I was carrying his jacket and my bag. There was a lot of stuff we were juggling, trying to go through this narrow aisle to get into our seats. He was continually bumping his elbow and in a lot of pain. He was grumbling; I was grumbling.

I had been telling him, "Father Benedict, please let this be like our last big trip. You don't need to do this anymore. You know, people could watch you on EWTN or listen to your tapes or whatever."

A few minutes later I asked, "Father Benedict, how are you doing?" He replied, "Oh, I'm miserable." So I said, "Yeah, I'm miserable too. Please, Father Benedict, remember how you feel right now the next time somebody calls and asks you, like to travel to California or something."

He said, "Okay…Yeah."

So we had this beautiful retreat with some priests out in Michigan. We got back on the plane to fly home. Then he turned to me and said, "WASN'T THIS A GREAT TRIP!?"

Father Benedict set aside the suffering for the spiritual value of the retreat and for the people who came. He focused on what was good, on what God was doing, on what was positive, and he was able to overcome his own sufferings. It's an example for us to follow.

Books by
Father Benedict Groeschel, CFR

- *God and Us,* Daughters of St. Paul (January 1982)
- *Listening at Prayer,* Paulist Press; 3rd edition (March 1984)
- *Spiritual Passages: The Psychology of Spiritual Development "for those who seek,"* Crossroad Publishing (December 1984)
- *The Courage to be Chaste,* Paulist Press (September 1985)
- *Stumbling Blocks or Stepping Stones: Spiritual Answers to Psychological Questions,* Paulist Press (January 1987)
- *Thy Will Be Done: A Spiritual Portrait of Terence Cardinal Cooke,* Alba House (September 1990)
- *The Reform of Renewal,* Ignatius Press (October 1990)
- *A Still, Small Voice: A Practical Guide on Reported Revelations,* Ignatius Press (February 1993)
- *Healing the Original Wound: Reflections on the Full Meaning of Salvation,* Servant Publications (July 1993)

- *Heaven in Our Hands: Living the Beatitudes: Receiving the Blessings You Long For*, Servant Books (August 1994)
- *Augustine: Major Writings*, Crossroad Publishing (April 1995)
- *Arise from Darkness: What to Do When Life Doesn't Make Sense*, Ignatius Press (December 1995)
- *In the Presence of Our Lord: The History, Theology, and Psychology of Eucharistic Devotion*, Our Sunday Visitor (March 1997)
- *A Priest Forever: The Life of Father Eugene Hamilton*, Our Sunday Visitor (March 1998)
- *Quiet Moments with Padre Pio: 120 Daily Readings*, Charis Books (January 1999)
- *Praying in the Presence of Our Lord: Prayers For Eucharistic Adoration,* Our Sunday Visitor (March 1999)
- *The Journey toward God: In the Footsteps of the Great Spiritual Writers-Catholic, Protestant, and Orthodox*, Servant Books (March 2000)
- *Quiet Moments with Benedict Groeschel: 120 Daily Readings*, Servant Books (September 2000)

Books by Father Benedict Groeschel, CFR

- *Praying in the presence of the Lord with the Saints*, Our Sunday Visitor (January 2001)
- *Behold He Comes: Meditations on the Incarnation: Daily Readings from Advent to Epiphany*, Servant Books (August 2001)
- *From Scandal to Hope*, Our Sunday Visitor (January 2002)
- *The Cross at Ground Zero*, Our Sunday Visitor (February 2002)
- *The King Crucified and Risen: Meditations on the Passion and Glory of Christ (Daily Readings from Ash Wednesday to Divine Mercy Sunday*, Servant Books (October 2002)
- *The Rosary: Chain of Hope (Meditations on the Mysteries of the Rosary with Twenty Renaissance Paintings)*, Ignatius Press (May 2003)
- *There are No Accidents: In All Things Trust in God*, Our Sunday Visitor (May 2004)
- *Praying to Our Lord Jesus Christ: Prayers and Meditations through the Centuries*, Ignatius Press (November 2004)
- *Why Do We Believe? (Strengthening Your Faith in Christ)*, Our Sunday Visitor (January 2005)

- *A Drama of Reform*, Ignatius Press (October 2005)
- *The Virtue Driven Life*, Our Sunday Visitor (September 2006)
- *Praying with the Creed: Meditations from the Oratory*, Our Sunday Visitor (April 2007)
- *Questions and Answers About Your Journey to God*, Our Sunday Visitor (September 2007)
- *Everyday Encounters With God: What Our Experiences Teach Us about the Divine*, Word Among Us Press (April 2008)
- *Experiencing the Mystery of Christ: Meditations from the Oratory*, Our Sunday Visitor (May 2008)
- *Tears of God: Persevering in the Face of Great Sorrow or Catastrophe*, Ignatius Press (February 2009)
- *After This Life: What Catholics Believe About What Happens*, Our Sunday Visitor (November 2009)
- *The Journey of Faith: How to Deepen Your Faith in God, Christ, and the Church*, Our Sunday Visitor (April 2010)

- *Praying Constantly: Bringing Your Faith to Life*, Our Sunday Visitor (September 2010)
- *Travelers Along The Way: The Men and Women who Shaped my Life,* Servant (October 2010)
- *I Am With You Always,* Ignatius Press (November 2010)
- *The Saints In My Life: My Favorite Spiritual Companions,* Our Sunday Visitor (October 2011)
- *Jesus and Mary: In Praise of their Glorious Names,* Our Sunday Visitor (September 2012)

Made in the USA
Middletown, DE
05 May 2023